CONFLICT AND MOOD

Conflict and Mood

FACTORS AFFECTING STABILITY OF RESPONSE

by Patricia Kendall
Bureau of Applied Social Research
Columbia University

THE FREE PRESS, GLENCOE, ILLINOIS

Printed in the United States of America

To Paul F.

and Robert K.

CONTENTS

INTRODUCTION

Problems of social change have commanded attention probably for as long as men have studied society. In most general terms, the central questions are these: what were the factors bringing about crucial developments in social, economic and political organization; and, once these developments had occurred, what were their consequences? The compelling character of these questions in the social sciences has made it especially important to devise adequate techniques for describing and studying processes of social change.

The development of methods has proceeded in two essentially different directions. On the one hand, social change has been studied through historical analysis. By examining chains of events, the historian attempts to trace the process which brought them into being and the effects which they then had. For example, what special conditions prevailed in the 16th Century which made the Reformation possible? What were the political consequences of the decision between Catholicism and Protestantism?

Comparative analysis has also been used in the exploration of social change. In his study of several historical situations which seem similar in some respects and different in others, the social historian, such as Max Weber in his comparative analysis of world religions, examines their respective social consequences. Neither the individual nor the comparative historical studies lend themselves to precise conclusions, however. Because so many factors operate in any situation, it is difficult to isolate the influence of any one.

Laboratory experiments approach questions of social change from an opposed point of view. Instead of studying complex situations or events, the experimenter generally evaluates the consequences of narrowly delimited experimental variations. For obvious reasons, the experimenter cannot manipulate social institutions or cultural traditions. He must therefore study the influence of his narrowly defined stimuli on limited spheres of behavior and attitude among relatively small groups. What he thus gains in precision he sacrifices by being forced to deal with relatively trivial problems. Furthermore, experimentation involves the study of changes under contrived conditions, which may have limited bearing on the complex conditions which ordinarily obtain.

In recent years a new method for the study of short-term social change has been developed. These *panel techniques*, as they are called, are based on repeated observations of the units under study over a period of several months or several years. When properly designed, a panel study combines some of the advantages of historical comparisons, on the one hand, and of laboratory experiments, on the other. It permits the study of fairly complex problems without the artificiality of the laboratory; it can achieve a degree of precision not usually possible in historical comparisons.

The central problem of this study does not call for a detailed analysis of panel techniques.[1] However, there are two features of special importance to our investigation. The first of these concerns the major operations in panel studies; the second deals with the notion of turnover.

Basic Operations in Panel Studies

The essential characteristic of panel techniques is the cross-analysis of observed behavior, attitudes or status attributes at successive points of time. Three major types of cross-analysis can be distinguished. First of all, we can characterize people according to certain sociological or psychological attributes and study the relative variability of their behavior or status. For example, we can separate potential voters into those who have reference groups with conflicting political orientations and those whose reference groups have similar orientations. We can then determine, as social psychological theory would lead us to suppose, whether vote intentions of those subject to conflicting orientations are more unstable (i.e., variable). The same formal procedures are also used in investigations of social mobility or shifts in status. For example, if we characterize recruits in training as being either conformist or non-conformist with regard to rules and regulations in the Army, we can then determine whether those who are most highly conformist during the early stages of their careers are more likely to be promoted later on.[2]

A second basic panel operation consists in relating observed changes in attitude or behavior to events which have occurred in the interval between successive observations. Or, which is only a reformulation of the same point, we can investigate whether those who were exposed to a particular influence exhibit changes in attitude or behavior which might be expected from the nature of their exposure. This type of analysis is relevant in studies dealing with receptiveness to new information or new cultural definitions. For example, do residents of a community in which there is a campaign of education about the United Nations develop different attitudes toward the UN?

The third basic operation involves a cross-analysis of changes in one attitude or behavior pattern and changes in another. The logic of this is applicable to problems dealing with strains toward consistency in the mores, on the social level, or progressive integration of personality patterns, on the individual level. If concerned with the integration of attitudes, for example, we might ask whether, as a politcal campaign progresses, individuals develop greater harmony between their vote intentions and their stands on relevant campaign issues. Do they resolve contradictions between what they think of a candidate and what they think of his position on important domestic and foreign policies?

Several studies have made use of repeated observations of individual characteristics or behavior. Psychologists, for example, have long been interested in changes in IQ level, and have carried out repeated tests with the same individuals.[3] Lewis M. Terman and his associates followed the careers of children who were considered particularly gifted, noting how they developed in later years.[4] The Gluecks restudied the men whose criminal careers they had previously investigated in an effort to learn whether there was any improvement in their conduct.[5] Still other studies making use of repeated observations will be found in the field of medical research, where groups of persons are kept under scrutiny for many years and examined periodically for the appearance or progress of particular medical symptoms.

Although these investigations made use of repeated observations, they were not genuine panel studies. In none was there systematic cross-analysis to isolate changes in particular individuals. Instead, the successive observations were generally used to trace *trends* in the behavior or characteristics of the group as a whole. What was reported in most cases was the *net* change for the total group under observation, rather than specific changes of particular individuals.

In the published literature, there are only two major studies of social change based on panel techniques. One of these[6] traced the development of vote intentions during the 1940 presidential campaign. Through modes of analysis described above, the analysts distinguished between different types of change in vote intention and between different effects of the campaign.

The People's Choice covered six months in a political campaign. The second major panel study continued over a longer period of time. In order to trace the influence of community pressures on attitudes and personality structure, Newcomb observed Bennington College students over a four year period.[7] He was able to show that the college community encouraged a uniformity of opinion among students. Students coming from families with political and economic orientations very different from those prevailing in the college community gradually developed attitudes corresponding to majority opinion on these matters. Newcomb was also able to specify the conditions - both social and psychological - which made for varying degrees of attitude change.[8]

We have said that the distinguishing characteristic of true panel studies is that they are based on the cross-analysis of observations obtained at different points of time. Let us see how this analysis actually proceeds. We shall start with the simplest kind of panel analysis, that relating answers of the same question asked at two different times.[9] The example which we shall use comes from a study of the 1948 presidential campaign.[10] In both the June and October interviews, panel members were asked, "Do you personally expect that this country will be in another great war within the next ten years or so, or do you think there is a good chance of avoiding it?" Table A presents the results of a cross-classification of June and October responses:

Table A

	June Interview		
October Interview	Expects war	Does not expect war	Total
Expects war	194	147	341
Does not expect war	45	211	256
Total	239	358	597

There are several points of interest in Table A. First of all, we notice that the number of people saying that they expected war increased between June and October. But we note, secondly, that even though there was an overall trend toward greater pessimism, there were some persons who became more optimistic. Further, the total number of "changers" - those shifting from one position to another - is greater than the net change. To some extent, shifts in one direction were countered by shifts in the opposite direction, so that the net change was not as large as the component changes would lead one to expect.

Three major problems are suggested by these facts. First of all, we should like to know why there was increased pessimism between the two interviews; that is, what influence intervened between June and October. A second problem concerns the characteristics of changers. Which kinds of persons are most susceptible to the influences bringing about greater pessimism? Are some groups affected by one influence, and other groups affected by very different events or situations? A final problem concerns the characteristics of those who behave contrary to the general trend. In other words, which types of people become more optimistic when the general drift of opinion is toward increased pessimism? This last problem is focused on individuals who resist prevailing pressures and influences.

This is the accepted pattern of panel analysis. Answers to repeated questions are cross-tabulated (or repeated observations compared); speculations regarding the observed marginal and internal changes are then explored through the basic operations which we have described.

The Notion of Turnover

Growing out of these procedures, central to the panel method, is a problem which, until now, has received no systematic study. Questions asked of an individual can be ranged along a continuum of susceptibility to change. At one extreme are questions dealing with the attributes of the respondent - his sex and race, for example. These are invariant characteristics; we expect, therefore, that questions about them will be answered in the same way on successive occasions. At the other extreme are questions about highly volatile opinions which can change in response to varied influences. Expectations regarding the possibility of war would be an example of what we have in mind here. The progress of conferences with representatives of the

Soviet Union, an incident in a former enemy country now jointly occupied by the United States and the Soviet Union, a report on Russia's military strength - all of these can greatly affect our opinions about the imminence of war. And since the opinion is one subject to so many influences, it would not surprise us to find that individuals give different answers when they are asked about their expectations on several occasions.

In between these two extremes is a third type of question, dealing with characteristics which, on theoretical grounds, seem less invariant than sex or race, but, at the same time, less volatile than opinions. These are characteristics which are generally considered "deep rooted" or "basic." We might include here, for example, religious beliefs, attitudes toward minority groups, general political and economic orientations, and so on. All of these attitudes can change; it is unlikely that they will, however, in response only to weak and shortlived influences. Newcomb's study suggests that the modification of political and economic attitudes is gradual, apparently requiring extended membership in a group which exerts strong pressures for uniformity.[11] Because of these considerations, we expect very little change in response when questions concerning these basic attitudes are repeated after relatively short intervals of time.

It turns out that this is not the case, however. When we examine answers to repeated questions dealing with so-called basic attitudes, we find as much variability as we did in connection with opinions about the possibility of war.[12] For example, recent studies have explored the possibility of determining basic personality needs and characteristics through what are essentially survey procedures.[13] From these efforts have come a number of "scales" measuring "authoritarianism," "prejudice," and so on. In a panel study, undertaken for quite different purposes,[14] a number of items from the authoritarianism scale were included. One of these asked the respondent whether he agreed or disagreed with the statement, "Prison is too good for sex criminals; they should be publicly whipped or worse."[15] Table B shows that, as with the example of a volatile opinion, there is considerable internal variation in response to this question:

Table B

May Interview	November Interview Agree	Disagree	Total
Agree	155	58	213
Disagree	63	161	224
Total	218	219	437

The point of essential similarity between Tables A and B is the frequency of internal variations. One conspicuous difference is that in the present case, the marginal distributions remain virtually constant between the two interviews; the number of persons shifting from "disagree" to "agree" is almost equal to the number of respondents changing from "agree" to "disagree." This is a general characteristic of the phenomenon which we are studying.

The result of Table B is not an isolated case. From a number of panel studies carried out within the last several years we were able to compile a varied collection of repeated questions with constant marginal distributions but considerable internal variation.

Up to this time, the phenomenon of turnover, as we shall call it, has generally been ascribed to chance factors and considered a function of "unreliability" of the measuring instrument.[16] However, it is precisely this assumption which is here being subjected to empirical and theoretical review. We have studied whether shifts in response, such as those observed in Table B, are attributable solely to chance factors.

Plan of the Investigation

In our efforts to find some explanation for the phenomenon of turnover in response to attitude and opinion questions, we have made use of two quite different sets of material.[17]

(1) *Existing panel studies:* We first examined existing panel studies from our special point of view.[18] Three large scale researches were available for this purpose. All of these were studies in which the Bureau of Applied Social Research of Columbia University had cooperated, and all were focused on problems of attitude change, although in very different substantive areas.

The study offering the most diverse and detailed materials was that carried out during the 1948 presidential campaign. Known as the Elmira Study, this panel was sponsored jointly by a committee representing several universities and organizations.[19] Like the earlier investigation on which it was modelled, the Elmira Study traced the development of definite vote intentions during the course of the campaign. The panel members were interviewed at four times, in June, August, October, and immediately after the election in November. In each of the pre-election interviews they were asked a variety of questions about their vote intentions, their images of the major candidates, their positions with regard to some of the main campaign issues, and their political activities. In the final interview the panel members were queried about their actual behavior on Election Day. While the Elmira Study contains results of great substantive interest, it also proved very useful in our somewhat different kind of analysis.

The second major panel study on which we have drawn was concerned with changes in attitudes toward and information about the United Nations. The Cincinnati Study, as it will be called, was designed to test the effectiveness of an educational campaign sponsored jointly by the American Association for the United Nations, the United Nations Association of Cincinnati and the Stephen H. Wilder Foundation of Cincinnati. The original study design did not call for panel techniques; these were introduced later by Columbia's Bureau of Applied Social Research. Just before the campaign got under way, in September of 1947, the National Opinion Research Center of the University of Chicago ascertained the level of information and the kinds of attitudes existing in Cincinnati at that time; six months later, when the campaign had come to an end, NORC investigated a second sample of respondents to determine what effect the educational materials had had.[20] At the same time that this second group of respondents was being studied, the Bureau conducted reinterviews with members of the first sample, using exactly the same schedule. While the material of the Cincinnati Study does not have the rich variety found in the Elmira Study, it too has contributed greatly at crucial points in our analysis.

Finally we were able to draw on a panel studying the impact of events in Palestine on attitudes toward Jews.[21] In November, 1947, a sample of individuals living in Baltimore, Md., were asked a series of questions which can be best described as adaptations of the items developed by the Berkeley group.[22] Respondents were asked mainly about their attitudes toward minority groups, the degree of their contact with these groups and evidences of authoritarian personality. In May of 1948, just after Israel had declared itself an independent state, it was decided to reinterview the white Christians in the original sample to see whether the formation of a Jewish state in any way modified previous attitudes toward Jews. The second schedule repeated some of the prejudice items from the first; in addition it included questions dealing with attitudes toward Palestine and information concerning events which had taken place there.

Of particular value was a series of supplementary interviews obtained from selected panel members in the Baltimore Study. Some months after the second formal interviews had been completed, approximately 70 respondents who had been especially variable in their responses to the poll questions were intensively interviewed about their reasons for change. Ideally, these interviews should have been conducted immediately after the second poll questionnaire had been administered so that the respondents could more easily remember why they had given different answers to the various questions. As our analysis at several points indicates, however, the intensive materials are highly suggestive.

Where we have used materials from existing panel studies, these have been drawn, by and large, from one or another of the investigations just described. At certain points, however, we shall find it helpful to make use of other panel studies which provide information not readily available in the Elmira, Cincinnati or Baltimore Studies. The nature of these supplementary investigations will be described in some detail at those points where they enter into analysis.

(2) *Systematic experimentation:* The second set of material was collected especially for our investigation of the factors affecting stability of response. Two of the factors suggested by our analysis of existing panel materials - conflict and mood - were selected for more intensive study.[23] After considerable refinement and reformulation of the hunches growing out of our previous analysis, we constructed two separate schedules, one designed to study the role of conflict, the other of mood changes, in producing unstable responses.[24]

Detailed description of the content of these questionnaires will be reserved for the chapters which follow.

There are, however, certain general features of the experiments which might be discussed here.

Our research design called for a test and retest with the same subjects. This need to locate the same persons a second time presented some difficulties; it meant that we had to take as our subjects persons whom we could expect to find in the same groups for a period of time. Such persons are not likely to be representative of the total population, however.[25] We explored the possibility of drawing our subjects from several atypical, but different, groups – college students, prison inmates, chronic patients in hospitals, members of organizations which held regular meetings, and so on. In this way we would have included in our sample persons of diverse occupational background, age, educational level, and so on. It soon became clear, however, that access to non-academic groups would not be easy to obtain. Consequently we were forced, somewhat reluctantly, to carry out our experiments with college students. This fact to some extent limits the generality of our results; older persons with less education might not react in the same way as our young students did to the situations presented them. We feel, however, that this limitation is less serious in our study than it might be in other investigations. We are concerned with the operation of factors which are not related, in any direct way, either to education or age. It seems fairly certain that the experience of finding it difficult to choose between equally attractive alternatives is a universal one. So, we would guess, is the tendency of attitude changes to parallel changes in mood.

In all there were approximately 1000 students from whom we obtained two interviews. About half of these, 553 to be exact, answered the questionnaire dealing with conflict situations; the remaining 513 filled out the schedule designed to study the relation between mood changes and attitude shifts. In order to introduce as much diversity as possible, we enlisted the cooperation of a number of different institutions. The subjects in the conflict study were students in the Department of Economics in the School of General Studies at Columbia and in the Department of Sociology at the University of Washington in Seattle. Students participating in the mood study were enrolled in the Departments of Sociology at Northwestern University, New Jersey College for Women, Smith College and the School of General Studies at Columbia University; and in the Department of Psychology at the University of Connecticut.

Because of our limited resources, it was impossible to employ field techniques in these experimental studies. Our schedules were self-administered, as "paper-and-pencil" tests. Each subject filled in his answers on the blank form, returning it when he was finished. Self-administered questionnaires have several disadvantages: one of these is that it is impossible to observe the reactions or behavior of the subject as he answers the questions; a second is that it is impossible to clarify any points of confusion unless the subject himself raises questions. But self-administration has one great advantage which, in the present case, perhaps outweighed the disadvantages. It eliminates the possible influence of interviewer bias.

The schedules were given out during the regular class meetings of the courses, with the second or retest coming approximately four weeks after the first. At no time were the subjects informed of the real purpose of the studies;[26] nor were they told, prior to the administration of the retest, that they would be asked to fill out the same schedule on two separate occasions. In neither study were the subjects asked to sign their names; in fact, the anonymous character of the responses was emphasized.[27]

So far as possible, the different groups of students received standard instructions. The most important of these were written out on the face sheet of the schedules themselves, and the students were cautioned to read them carefully. In addition, we prepared a set of instructions for the persons administering the schedules; these included preferred answers if subjects questioned the purpose of the study, if they asked exactly what they were supposed to do, and so on.

* * * *

The report has been divided into three main sections. Chapters 1 and 2 present our findings on the two major topics which we investigated - the role of conflict and of mood changes in producing unstables responses. The data used in these chapters come both from existing studies and from those especially developed for our purposes.

Chapter 3 considers other factors which seem to bring about turnover. One section deals with the role of interest and concern; a second presents some evidence to show that the nature of the questioning procedure plays a part in making for unstable responses. By and large, the analysis of this chapter is based on the examination of existing panel studies.

There are, finally, a number of appendices. These deal with certain technical problems, and include additional findings not considered appropriate for the main body of the report.

Procedural Problems

There were two procedural problems which we met in all phases of our analysis. The first problem was what *index of turnover* to use, so that the relative instability of answers to different questions could be compared. The second dealt with the general *scheme of analysis* to be followed.

The turnover index which we finally adopted was one which, in the light of theoretical considerations, seemed preferable to others which might have been used.[28] For the sake of illustration, we can report that its value in Table B is .16, obtained in the following way. The *smaller* of the turnover cells was expressed as a proportion of the total sample - 13 percent. The same was done for the marginal totals corresponding to that smaller turnover cell - the 219 individuals who disagreed with the statement about sex criminals in November and the 213 who agreed with it in May. These two percentages were 50 and 49 respectively. The turnover index is:

$$\begin{aligned} x &= \tfrac{1}{2}\,(.50 + .49) - \tfrac{1}{2}\left[(.50 + .49)^2 - 4\,(.13)\right]^{\frac{1}{2}} \\ &= .16 \end{aligned}$$

We can interpret this figure intuitively as the probability than an individual will change his response. The index has a lower limit of 0, when there are no cases in one or both of the turnover cells, and an upper limit of .50, when the cross-tabulation of answers obtained from the repeated question reveals no relationship at all. As we shall see, the index value usually varies between .05 and .10, although occasionally it is as high as .30.[29]

The pattern of analysis which we used can best be introduced through a concrete example. In a later section of our study[30] it will turn out that the difficulty of questions in an interview seems to be of central importance in producing turnover. Without defining "difficulty" any more precisely at the present time and without explaining how it is related to instability of response, let us see how we went about studying its influence.

First of all, we presented our subjects with a variety of choice situations, which were posed in two interviews conducted approximately one month apart. We asked them, for example, whether they would prefer a job with high pay or one with security; we asked them whether or not they would help a friend during a college examination; and so on. In each case the subjects were required to make a decision between the two alternatives. Since the questions were repeated, we could determine which respondents made the same choice in both interviews and which shifted from one alternative to the other.

In addition to choosing one of the alternatives, the subjects were asked to indicate in each case how much difficulty they had experienced in reaching the decision. In analyzing any of these questions, then, the crucial problem is whether those who reported marked difficulty show a greater degree of turnover than those who reported little difficulty.

For our concrete example we have chosen an item dealing with relatively simple preferences: "If you had your choice, would you prefer to spend your vacation at the seashore or in the mountains?" The first step in our analysis is to distinguish those who reported that the question was difficult to answer and those who reported no trouble. The second step is to see which group has a higher degree of turnover in vacation preferences between the first and second interviews. There are a number of points to be noted in Table C. First of all, the marginals are quite constant in both of the difficulty groups. The proportion of those saying they would prefer to vacation at the seashore is virtually the same in both interviews. But it is not always the same people who express a preference for the seashore. We see in both parts of Table C that some respondents vacillate between the alternatives. Most importantly, the degree of vacillation is greater among those who reported that they had difficulty in arriving at the required decision; this is indicated in the higher index value of this first group.

This is the pattern of analysis which we shall follow in a large part of our study. We shall divide the total sample according to some criterion which we hypothesize will operate to produce more or less turnover; within each of the groups obtained in this way we shall study the stability

Table C

The respondents reporting difficulty in making a decision are more unstable in their vacation preferences than are those reporting little difficulty.

	Experienced "great" or "medium" difficulty in reaching a decision			Experienced "little" difficulty in reaching a decision		
	Interview I			Interview I		
Interview II	Seashore	Mountains	Total	Seashore	Mountains	Total
Seashore	54	14	68	155	6	161
Mountains	12	34	46	11	125	136
Total	66	48	114	166	131	297
	Turnover index:		.14	Turnover index:		.02

of responses to repeated questions. In the present instance, the criterion was reported difficulties in answering the question. In other cases we shall divide the sample according to their answers to other questions, according to their background characteristics, and so on. In still other cases we shall make a somewhat different kind of comparison. Instead of contrasting the behavior of two groups in their successive answers to the same question, we shall study the behavior of a single group in answer to several questions. In all of these, our goal will be to find factors related to varying degrees of turnover.

Thus far we have focused attention on *amount* of turnover. There will be other occasions, however, when we will be primarily interested in the *direction* of turnover.[31] In these cases we shall not compute a value for the turnover index, which is essentially a measure of amount of turnover. Instead, we shall compare the types of respondents who shift from, let us say, preferences for the seashore to preferences for the mountains with the kinds of subjects who shift in the opposite direction. As we shall see in later chapters, this kind of analysis can also be revealing.

While we do not claim that our study is exhaustive, in the sense of explaining all turnover, we have been able to isolate a limited number of factors which explain a phenomenon previously considered the result of chance alone.

CHAPTER 1

ROLE OF CONFLICT

A first factor affecting stability of response was suggested by the difficulties which some respondents experience in answering survey questions. By their comments and their behavior, many indicate that they find it hard to choose among the alternatives presented to them.

Some sources of this difficulty are familiar. When the stated alternatives are not mutually exclusive, or when the list of responses is not exhaustive, survey respondents often find themselves unable to select among the different possibilities offered them.

The difficulties of which we speak here, however, are somewhat different. They seem to stem from some sort of *psychological conflict* created by the question or the interview situation. The respondents appear to *experience certain questions as requesting a choice between beliefs held with equal firmness or between values considered equally sacred.* Such requests are obviously difficult to fill.

I. ANALYSIS OF EXISTING PANEL MATERIALS

Analysis of existing survey materials, more especially of existing panel data, permits a preliminary investigation of the role of conflict in producing unstable responses.

There will be no attempt in the present section to analyze with any great precision the process relating conflict and response instability. The whole matter, it turns out, is quite complicated, and will receive detailed attention in the second section of this chapter. The present review is intended as a descriptive one, distinguishing some of the different situations which might be considered conducive to psychological conflict.

Conflict of Means

One type of conflict situation comes about when the respondent has in mind a specific goal but is not sure of the best *means* for achieving it. Each alternative seems to offer both advantages and disadvantages. Conflict arises when one policy precludes or is contradictory to the other.

Let us illustrate this with a concrete example from the Cincinnati Study. Respondents were asked whether they expected war within the next ten years.[1] While we can assume that all will want to prevent war, it is safe to say that those who answer that they expect war will be especially concerned with this goal. But what are the means to achieve it? One possibility would be to strengthen the United States by building up defensive and offensive forces; this course might have the disadvantage, however, of increasing suspicion among other nations. An alternative policy would be to institute an effective system for the international control of armaments.[2] This might lessen the possibility of war, but it would also have the disadvantage of weakening the military position of the United States. Basically, then, the most obvious courses of action seem contradictory to each other. And since it is not at all clear which is preferable, in terms of relative advantages and disadvantages, we can predict that those who are especially concerned with achieving the goal will experience great difficulties in deciding between them.

There is actually some evidence for this in the Cincinnati Study. While there was no question asking for a decision between strengthening the United States, on the one hand, and strengthening international controls, on the other, one item did inquire into attitudes toward international control of the atom bomb.[3] Approval of such international control can be taken as implying support for an international system or organization; disapproval as meaning support for policies strengthening the United States. Those who are especially concerned with the prevention of war manifest their difficulties by their inability to state consistently which of the two policies seems preferable.

It was necessary to control education here because of the varying expectations of different educational groups. (The lower educated are more pessimistic.) Within each of the educational groups, however, we find that those who are especially concerned with the prevention of war experience the question on control of atom bombs as a request to choose between two alternatives, each of which has advantages and disadvantages. They respond to this request with a higher degree of instability.

Table 1

Those who expect war within the next ten years are less stable in their approval or disapproval of international control of the atom bomb.

(Cincinnati Study)

	Index Value	Number of Cases
High Education		
Expect war	.10	66
Do not expect war	.08	84
Low Education		
Expect war	.19	133
Do not expect war	.08	81

Conflict of Goals

Indecision concerning the best means to achieve a goal held firmly in mind is probably not so common as indecision concerning the goals themselves. Do we want to teach or do research? Psychological conflict arises when the two goals are incompatible, when teaching precludes research or doing research makes teaching impossible. And, according to our expectations, this conflict will reflect itself in the respondent's inability to make a stable choice between these two goals.

There were no questions in the available panel studies which permitted exactly the kind of analysis required to determine whether these expectations are borne out. Nonetheless there was one item in the Elmira Study which provides some evidence. Respondents were asked their attitudes toward labor unions:

With which of these four statements do you come closest to agreeing?

(1) Labor unions in this country are doing a fine job.

(2) While they do make some mistakes, on the whole labor unions are doing more good than harm.

(3) Although we need labor unions in this country, they do more harm than good the way they are run now.

(4) This country would be better off without any labor unions at all.

Those who select the first alternative are clearly pro-union in attitude. They are not indecisive about the continued existence of unions. Nor are the respondents who select the fourth alternative; they are as definite in their opposition as the first group was in its support. But what of the individuals selecting the two middle alternatives? Recasting these statements, both imply indecision about the goal of strengthening or supporting labor unions. In each, arguments indicating that the respondent wants to see the goal achieved are countered by arguments suggesting that he does not want its achievement. In the first of the statements the balance of the arguments in pro-union; in the second it is anti-union. But both are indecisive.

The consequence of this indecision is revealed in the inability of respondents selecting either of the two middle statements to express a consistent attitude toward labor unions. This is seen when their responses to a second repeated question dealing with unions are studied. The panel members were asked, in June and October, whether they thought there were any groups which "are getting more power anywhere in the United States than is good for the country." Among the groups listed were labor unions. Table 2 studies the consistency with which this group was selected among those who, on the previous question, expressed pro-union, anti-union or indecisive attitudes.

The differences are by no means large, but they suggest that one consequence of indecision, or goal conflict as we have called it here, is instability of response.

Table 2

Those who have indecisive attitudes toward labor unions are less consistent in selecting unions as groups which have too much power.

(Elmira Study)

	Index Value	Number of Cases
Unions are doing a fine job	.06	103
The country would be better off without unions	.05	54
Indecisive attitude	.10	618

This finding bears an interesting relationship to the work of Guttman and Suchman. They have found[4] that there is a curvilinear relationship between position on an attitude continuum and the intensity with which the attitude is held. This relationship is U-shaped: those at the extremes of the continuum hold the attitude with greater intensity than do those in a middle position. The present finding suggests that there is a curvilinear relationship between position on an attitude continuum and *stability* of response. But the relationship is exactly opposite to the intensity curve. We expect that those who are at the extremes will be most stable, while those in a middle position will be least so. The two findings might be considered complementary.

Conflict of Ideology and Attitude

Another type of conflict situation seems to arise when there is a discrepancy between private attitudes and public ideology. We might consider this a variant of goal conflict in the sense that the individual wants to conform to the social norms specified in the ideology; but he wants at the same time to behave in the way implied by his attitude.

There is one group of respondents in whom it is particularly easy to see this type of conflict. These are the persons who, on the one hand, are prejudiced but who, on the other hand, accept the tenets of the so-called American Credo. Social researchers have long been aware of this conflict, and, indeed, when they investigate an area on which there are "good" and "bad" opinions, they spend much time planning the study design so that respondents will be able to express their true, rather than the socially acceptable, attitude.

When the problem is stated in this way it seems to be one of validity alone. Actually, however, it probably is not as simple as this. It is not likely that the only problem is one of concealing the socially unacceptable attitude, thereby giving an invalid response. What is more probable is that the prejudiced individual experiences a real conflict; he holds certain negative attitudes toward minority groups, and at the same time he believes, and truly believes, that such attitudes are wrong. On the assumption that there is this conflict, we should expect the prejudiced individual to give less stable responses. For he is in the position of having multiple and contradictory responses to the same issue.

Unfortunately none of the panel materials permitted us to study this question statistically. There was no way to classify the respondents according to their level of prejudice and then to see whether, on independent but related questions, there was a relationship between degree of prejudice and amount of turnover.

The qualitative materials of the Baltimore Study are very suggestive on this point, however. This investigation, centering as it did on the sensitive topic of anti-minority prejudice, met with more resistance than do most. When interviewers returned to the panel members for the second poll questionnaire, many met with rather violent refusals; and when respondents were approached for a third time to be interviewed intensively, many became extremely aggressive. Much of this reaction seemed to revolve around the difficulty, and perhaps in some cases the traumatic character, of answering a large variety of questions in which this conflict between "right" and "wrong" answers was involved. One of the best statements of this difficulty is contained in the following excerpt:

> *I hated to keep committing myself.* Nothing but questions about Jews. I just feel like it's a Jewish set-up and *I don't like to commit myself.* When it comes to human beings, *little opinions we have we like to keep to ourselves.* I don't hate anybody. The people we feel we can't get along with we stay away from. *When you express your opinions about human beings, it's tough.* I've known some very nice Jews. Couldn't be finer. I mind my own business and they mind theirs. I don't like to see them persecuted. *You couldn't be mean to old men and women and little children; yet I wouldn't want to mix with them.* Now you take the poorer sections of town. *You find colored people and Jews living in the same house even.* Now you or I wouldn't want to live in a house with colored people. But they don't seem to mind. Somehow or other, *they try to belittle you.* They try to make you feel like servants. Yet I know some Jewish businessmen who's good as gold and would try to push you to the top. *But I wouldn't want to say anything that would hurt anybody...*

This is a particularly rich comment, and therefore it will be analyzed in some detail. The respondent, first of all, makes repeated references to the discomfort experienced in being asked to commit himself; these we may take as indications of the conflict he experienced. And the source of this conflict is not hard to determine when the rest of the comment is examined. The first concrete reference to minority groups is a rather stereotyped statement that he has known some very fine Jews. This is followed by what appears to be a sincere expression of pity for those who have been persecuted. But this sympathetic sentiment is qualified by the first anti-Jewish comment: the respondent does not want to mix with Jews. His reasons are quite explicit - Jews don't mind living with colored people. But then, as is so frequently the case among prejudiced people, the next statement seems to contradict the preceding one. Jews make themselves inferior by living in close association with colored people; at the same time, they act superior and try to make others "feel like servants." This anti-Semitic outburst, if it can be called that, is again qualified. The respondent has known some fine Jewish businessmen who try to help others. The section of the interview which we have quoted ends on virtually the same note with which it began - the informant doesn't want to say anything that would hurt anybody.

It is not difficult to see how a conflict such as this between tolerance and anti-Semitism can lead to unstable responses in answer to repeated questions. Even within one paragraph, the respondent states many contradictory attitudes.

In another interview the conflict between the anti-minority sentiment and those reactions prescribed by the American Credo is even more explicitly stated. The respondent starts out by assuring the interviewer of his lack of prejudice:

> I make a big effort to be absolutely unbiased about everything. I think that's the best way to look at everything, if you can.

But these efforts are not always successful. Several moments later in the interview this same respondent is describing Jews in the following manner:

> I'm afraid I would have to say that they are over-aggressive and over-confident and somewhat loud. I don't believe I have ever seen a shy, retiring one in my life...They seem to have an uncanny ability to rate merchandise. I don't think they are too fond of physical labor. I never saw a Jew who was a steel worker...

Note that the respondent prefaces his negative remarks with the phrase, "I'm afraid I would have to say...", indicating his reluctance to say the "wrong" thing. After continuing in this vein for some time, he interrupts himself to comment:

> I guess a lot of this stuff sounds contradictory. (What do you mean?) It sounds as if I'm prejudiced on some of the answers and not on others. But we have some Jewish friends who are real nice people. What is this poll for? Is it for the same people as the last poll?

The respondent himself recognizes the contradiction between what his "efforts to be unbiased" would lead him to say, and what he is "afraid he has to say." He vacillates back and forth between stereotyped lack of prejudice ("we have some Jewish friends who are real nice people") and relatively overt anti-Semitism. And when there are these vacillations and contradictions *within* the interview, it is not hard to understand the way in which responses shift from one interview to the next. Instability is almost inevitable when the individual holds irreconcilable attitudes.

Conflicting Loyalties

Other individuals experience a conflict, not between abstract ideas or ideals, but rather because of the pressures of competing loyalties.

The modern adult belongs to or identifies with many social groups. He belongs to an occupational group; in all probability he still belongs to a family group with which he shares friends and social life; he may be a member of other groups as well - unions, church organizations, clubs of one kind or another. In addition he will identify with a number of social groups, more broadly defined, depending on his class status, his age, his sex, perhaps his nationality, and so on. Each of these groups imposes its own norms and standards - each of them expects, however implicitly, that the individual member will hold a specified attitude toward Jews, Negroes, Catholics, Russia, control of the atom bomb, and so on. For many persons these various norms will be in harmony with each other: What is expected of the individual, because of membership in a particular professional group, will coincide with the teachings of his church. But for perhaps an increasingly large number of persons, social groups which are of significance in their daily lives make conflicting demands or have contradictory norms.[5]

One of the respondents interviewed intensively in the Baltimore Study stated this problem very succinctly:

> You know, *there was one of my best friends who was a Jew.* He was my father's best friend. He was a *business associate.* The only trouble was, *we didn't see each other in each other's homes.* And he was one of the finest men you could depend on. *In fact, I did depend on him often.* I'm proud

> of that friendship and I've told many people so. *The only trouble was, and it was something that Mr. Schwartz always said, we never met after 6 o'clock.* He was an internationalist of sorts. But his wife, she didn't progress with him. She was like an immigrant. She was not educated. Of course, Mr. Schwartz loved her just as much, and her sons loved her just as much. But she was one of those kind of women who never cared much about dress, etc, and it made for some hesitancy in going into their home. Her sons have wives who are just as American as our wives. Of course, they had no idea of being ashamed of their mother. *But it did make a certain barrier there, for going into their home.*

Mr. Schwartz was a business associate on whom one could depend, but there was no association after 6 o'clock. Putting this anecdote in different terms, we can say that the respondent, in his occupational role, had one attitude toward his Jewish friend; in the context of social relationships, his attitude was quite a different one.

The effects of these conflicting loyalties, or *cross-pressures,* as they have been called, are varied. It has been observed, for example, that persons who belong to groups with conflicting political orientations frequently do not vote in an election, or, if they do vote, they choose their candidate very late in the campaign.[6]

In addition to paralyzing the individual or delaying his decision, the experience of cross-pressures results in vacillation. This, in turn, leads to shifting responses. One of the panel members in the Baltimore Study, for example, had originally agreed that "It would be a good idea if more business firms refused to hire Jews." When this question was repeated in the intensive interview, the respondent said:

> Do we have to go into that again? Lots of people can't get along with Jews, but I wouldn't say that they shouldn't hire them. I wouldn't want to work for them. My boss was Jewish and he's the most wonderful man you ever met. *But I don't want to mix with him after work.* I wouldn't want to be in an office full of them; I don't think I'd care for that. (Well, do you agree or disagree with the statement?) *Well, I'll say no. I just don't care to work with them. Other than that I don't care.* I get along with them fine. My boss, the man I used to work for, was Jewish, and we were good friends. (The last time you said "yes," that you agreed with that statement.) Well, I don't like to say anything bad about anybody. I have nothing against them. I don't have anything against any Jew personally. I just wouldn't want to work in an office full of them. *I wouldn't want to keep anyone out of a job,* but I wouldn't want to be the only Gentile in an office full of Jews. (Why not?) Well, you know what I mean, they're overbearing. They act so superior, treat you like a servant. (Why do you think you might have agreed to that statement last time?) Well, I've known very nice Jewish people, but still - - well, I might have said "yes" because I wouldn't want to see them getting in all over. *But I really think it's all right as long as I don't have to work with them.*

When thinking of herself as a prospective employee who would have a variety of social contacts with her co-workers, this respondent is in favor of discriminating against Jews. When talking as a "human being," of whom certain sympathetic attitudes are expected, her expressed sentiments are more liberal.

This relationship between conflicting loyalties and instability of response is also revealed in the statistical materials of existing panel studies. The Elmira Study, we recall, was patterned after a study carried out during the 1940 presidential campaign. In the Sandusky Study, as we shall call it, the background characteristics of each respondent were studied to note whether he was affiliated with groups which had conflicting political orientations.

Thus a rich Catholic was assumed to be experiencing cross-pressures. So was a young worker who came from a traditionally Republican family. Each respondent was assigned a score value, corresponding to the number of conflict situations found to be present in his political environment. When these materials are examined, it develops that turnover in vote intention[7] is directly proportional to the number of cross-pressures experienced:

Table 3

Those who experience cross-pressures in their political environments are less stable in vote intention.

(Sandusky Study)

	Index Value	Number of Cases
No cross-pressures	.07	66
One cross-pressure	.08	185
Two or more cross-pressures	.15	121

Individuals who find themselves pulled in different directions have a difficult time deciding definitely whether or not they will vote; their intentions waver back and forth.

Very much the same result emerged from an entirely different kind of analysis. Early in World War II, the American Institute of Public Opinion conducted a panel study concerned mainly with levels of public morale. Two interviews were carried out, the first during the latter part of December, 1941, the second during June, 1942. One of the questions asked at both times was, "So far, are you satisfied or dissatisfied with the government's conduct of the war against Japan?" By and large, the majority expressed satisfaction. But there were some respondents who, presumably, were under cross-pressures when asked this question - the persons who had voted for Wendell Willkie in 1940. As Republicans, they were probably predisposed to criticize the government which had defeated their candidate. As loyal Americans, however, eager to see the United

States win the war against Japan and anxious to help toward that end, they were probably reluctant to make any critical statements. They thus experienced a conflict between their political and patriotic affiliations. This expressed itself in a greater degree of turnover when their responses to the question quoted above were compared with those of Democratic voters.

Table 4

Those who experienced cross-pressures between their patriotism and political partisanship are less stable in attitudes toward conduct of the war

(AIPO Study)

	Index Value	Number of Cases
Voted for Willkie in 1940	.18	273
Voted for Roosevelt in 1940	.08	316

That it was this conflict between patriotism and political attitude which made for greater turnover among the Republican voters is further indicated by the fact that, when asked a question about domestic policy ("Do you approve or disapprove of FDR's policies here at home?"), the Republicans were more stable than they had been in connection with the question of military policies, while the Democratic voters had exactly the same amount of turnover.[8]

Through a combination of qualitative materials and a few statistical results from existing studies, it has been possible to see that psychological conflict produces unstable responses. It now seems appropriate to examine the process more carefully, and to submit it to more rigorous test. For these purposes, special experiments were devised and carried out.

II. SYSTEMATIC EXPERIMENTATION

When the meaning of "conflict situations" is specified more precisely, we find that we are dealing essentially with problems of *decision formation*. The persons described previously as experiencing conflict did so in the sense of being unable to decide between alternative objectives or alternative courses of action.

Human beings are constantly required to make decisions. Some of these are relatively trivial; for example, decisions about how to spend one's leisure time, decisions between specific literary and musical works, and so on. Other decisions are more far-reaching in their implications for the individual. What career should he choose? Should he marry now, or wait until he is better established financially?

The psychological process by which individuals arrive at these decisions is only now becoming the object of intensive study. On the one hand, attempts are being made to set up mathematical models of the ways in which decisions can be reached. In addition, through the observation of small groups, psychologists are trying to determine the general laws of interaction by which a group reaches a decision.

None of these efforts has yet produced more than preliminary insights. When we talk about decision-making, therefore, we are forced to rely on more or less common-sense propositions, rather than being able to derive hypotheses from rigorously stated laws of behavior. One such common sense proposition about decision-making, basic to the expermental study of conflict, can be stated in the following ways:

> If an individual is asked to make a decision between two alternatives which, according to some relevant criterion, are of equal value, he will experience difficulty in making the choice. Stated differently, if the individual sees no difference between the two alternatives, he will be unable to decide between them.[9]

The relevance of this general proposition for a study of turnover is not obvious until its implications are considered. What are the consequences of being asked to choose between two equally desirable (or equally weighted) alternatives? One solution of the dilemma is not to make the decision at all. If the individual cannot decide whether to vote for Candidate X or Candidate Y, he may not vote at all.

Running out of the field, so to speak, provides one

possible escape from the dilemma. It is a solution which is probably adopted more frequently than is generally recognized. But what if this escape is blocked for one reason or another; what happens when the individual is *required* to choose between equivalent alternatives? Expectations regarding the outcome of that situation can again be stated in fairly common-sense terms:

> If the individual is forced to choose between two alternatives which seem to him of equal value, his decision will be an unstable one. That is, he will waver back and forth between one alternative and the other.[10]

Essentially, then, there are three major variables:

(1) *Instability of response (turnover):* Why is it that, under certain conditions, respondents vacillate in their answers to repeated questions? This is the phenomenon we are trying to explain; it is the dependent variable in the analysis.

(2) *Equivalence of the alternatives:* It is our hypothesis, to be explored in the following pages, that when individuals are forced to choose between equivalent (or substitutable) alternatives, their responses are unstable. In other words, equivalence might be considered the independent variable in this investigation.

(3) *Difficulty of the required decision:* According to our expectations, the more nearly equivalent the alternatives, the more difficult the task of choosing between them. And, in turn, the more difficult the decision, the greater the degree of turnover. Difficulty of the decision thus serves as a link between equivalence and instability of response: it is an "intervening variable."[11]

There are thus three basic relationships to be explored. First of all, is equivalence of the alternatives in fact related to difficulties in choosing between them? Turning to a second part of the chain, is this same equivalence related to instability of response? Finally, do those who have experienced difficulties make less stable choices?

Before turning to the material, however, it might be appropriate to clarify these major variables. The notion of turnover is by now familiar enough so that it need not detain us here. But what of "equivalence of alternatives" and "difficulty of the decision?"

Experimental Modification of Decision Dilemmas

The phrase "equivalent alternatives" is somewhat ambiguous. It may refer to the similar weight of physical objects; in the terms of the economist it may refer to the relative utilities of specific commodities; it may refer to the importance or value attached to possible courses of action; and so on.

Had there been a general interest in the problem of what happens when persons are forced to choose between equivalent alternatives, a variety of experimental situations might have been constructed. We might have observed the reactions of individuals to weight-lifting situations, to commands that they express their preferences for specific objects which are placed before them, and so on.

Our interest was not a general one, however. The purpose of this experiment was to see whether a phenomenon observed in the analysis of repeated interviews could be explained. Because of this, the experiment has been limited to what is possible within the context of a questionnaire; as a further limitation, the questions which have been used correspond, by and large, to those which are asked in public opinion surveys.[12]

Even within these restrictions, there is still considerable latitude for experimentation:

(1) We can create a variety of decision dilemmas according to the content of the alternatives which we make equivalent.

(2) We can make the decision dilemma more or less severe by varying the relative attractiveness of the alternatives.

(3) We can study the severity of the dilemma in groups with varying predispositions to find the alternatives equivalent.

Finally, methods for gauging the equivalence of different alternatives will be considered.

(1) *Types of decision dilemmas:* In the first section of this chapter, it was suggested that there are at least four types of dilemmas: the best means of achieving a stated goal, the more desirable of two incompatible goals, the discrepancy between experienced feelings or beliefs and accepted ideologies, the more compelling of conflicting loyalties. Upon closer analysis, it appears that, if "goals" are defined broadly enough to encompass anything the individual wants to do or achieve, the last two types become special instances of goal dilemmas. There is then a basic distinction between *goal* and *means* dilemmas.

The present study has been focused almost entirely on goal dilemmas: of the 18 questions calling for a decision between alternatives,[13] all but three involved some kind of goal dilemma. In some instances, we forced the respondent to indicate which of two competing *needs* he wanted most to satisfy. Thus we asked:

> When we think of the ideal kind of job, most of us would probably agree that we want a secure job which is important and well-paying at the same time. But sometime during their lives many people have to choose between a *secure* job which would *never* be well-paying or a *well-paying* job which is not and *never* will be secure. If you were offered two jobs, *equally interesting and important,* which do you think you would choose?
>
> -- I would choose the *secure* job, even though it never will pay well.
>
> -- I would choose the *well-paying* job, even though it is not and never will be secure. (AD, 2)[14]

Additional goal dilemmas were created by requiring the respondent to choose between conflicting *ideals*. For instance,

> Sometimes we have a conflict between our ideals. For example, we might find ourselves in a situation where our belief in freedom of speech was in conflict with our feeling of wanting to preserve American institutions which are dear to us.

> That might happen if you heard a speaker advocating the overthrow of our government. What would you recommend be done with the man?
>
> -- Allow him to speak even though he might influence some people to un-American behavior.
>
> -- Prevent him from speaking, even thought that would deprive him of his constitutional right to free speech. (BE, 4)

Defining goals and objectives in a rather loose sense, other dilemmas of this kind were created by asking for a decision between competing *preferences*. One example was the following:

> If you had your choice, would you prefer to spend your vacation at the seashore or in the mountains?
>
> -- At the seashore.
>
> -- In the mountains. (A-F, 27)

(Other examples of goal dilemmas will be reported in later sections of the analysis. The complete list is found in Appendix B.)

Although the schedule did not include any questions asking the respondents to choose between alternative *means*, it is perhaps worthwhile to say a word about how these dilemmas differ from those just considered. When talking of means dilemmas, we always assume that the objective is decided upon;[15] the dilemma arises in selecting the most effective methods for gaining the objective. Drawing on an earlier example, we would all agree that world peace is a most desirable objective. But what is the best method of maintaining peace? Should the United States fight, on a limited scale, to indicate our intentions of preventing the spread of Communism? Should all fighting, on whatever limited scale be avoided on the assumption that once fighting starts it can more easily develop into full scale war? The dilemma here is in deciding on the relative advantages and disadvantages of particular policies.

Goal and means dilemmas can be distinguished in the following way:

> *Goal dilemmas* come about when the individual expects that the gratification to be experienced through the attainment of one goal, G, is equal to the gratification to be experienced through the attainment of a second, and incompatible goal, $\bar{G}$.
>
> *Means dilemmas* come about when, given a particular goal, G, the individual believes that the ease of achieving G through one method, M, is equal to the ease of achieving G through a second and contradictory method, $\bar{M}$.

If this formulation is accepted, means dilemmas can perhaps be described as less "basic" than goal dilemmas. If we had perfect knowledge - if we could foresee all the consequences of a particular course of action - it would rarely be true that the same goal is equally attainable through alternative avenues. It is only because we do not know all of the consequences that the dilemma arises. The same is not true of goal dilemmas: no increase in our knowledge, no assumption of the perfect and rational human being, would enable us to escape the fact that individuals frequently desire things which are essentially incompatible.

There is a third major type of decision dilemma, different from those considered thusfar. There is no question of the relative desirability of goals or the ease of their attainment; the only problem is one of ability to *discriminate between objective stimuli*. The most clear-cut examples of this kind of dilemma are those mentioned previously in connection with psycho-physical discriminations; can the individual distinguish between two objects which weigh very nearly the same amount; can he tell the difference between two tones which are very similar; can he pick out the longer of two lines which are very nearly equal in length?

In questionnaire studies, this type of decision dilemma takes on a somewhat different form. Instead of being asked to make sensory discriminations, the individual is forced to make what might be called *cognitive distinctions*. In essence, however, the difficulties which he meets are exactly the same. Can he distinguish between a statement which is exactly true and one which is very nearly true? Can he tell the difference between two statements which are very similar in meaning? Can he discriminate between two words which differ only in the most subtle nuances? It is in problems of this kind that the questionnaire respondent meets the dilemma of cognitive discriminations. There were three questions in our study calling for distinctions of this kind:

> At the height of the war, how many men were there in the United States Army, 6,000,000 or 7,000,000? (CF, 29)
>
> When was the Battle of Gettysburg fought, July 1863, or September 1863? (AD, 30)
>
> What is the title of Charles Darwin's great work: "The Origin of Species" or "The Origin of the Species"? (BE,36)

It will develop that discriminations of this kind create exactly the same kind of dilemma that results from a request to distinguish between equally desirable goals.

(2) *Modification of decision dilemmas:* Three situations in which individuals can have difficulty choosing between offered alternatives have now been distinguished. But there is no indication, as yet, of how we can vary the severity of these dilemmas experimentally. Perhaps the best way of approaching this question is through the following scheme:

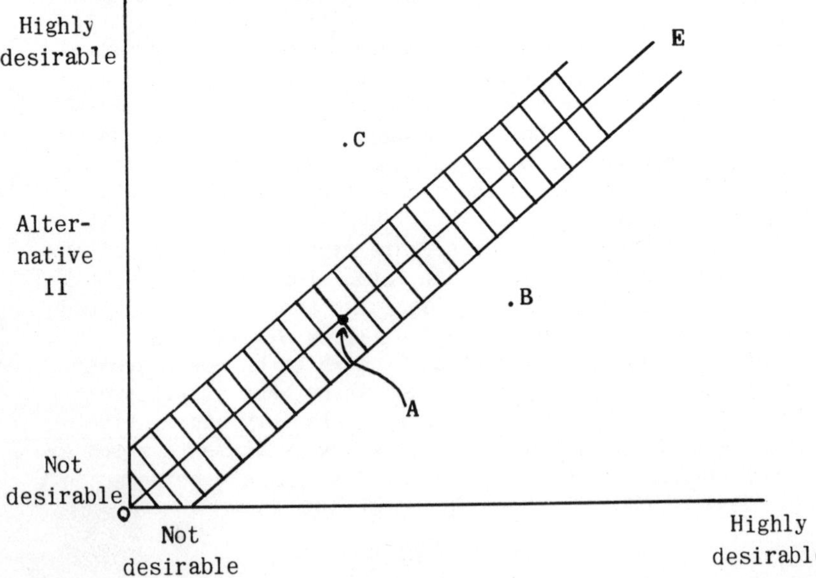

The axes of this diagram represent the desirability of two alternatives, which are considered simultaneously; each of the points, A, B and C, represents a *set* of two alternatives.

It is now possible to visualize the conditions under which a request to choose between two alternatives will present special difficulty. It is our expectation that the most severe dilemma will result when the two alternatives are equally desirable; in terms of this scheme, the most severe dilemmas will arise when the set of alternatives falls on the line, OE. We expect, further, that there will be a region of unknown width around this line where the alternatives are so nearly equal in desirability that decisions between them will be very difficult; this will be called the "region of equivalence."

The scheme also helps specify the ways in which the severity of decision dilemmas can be modified. This can be done by selecting sets of alternatives which are not balanced in strength or desirability, and which do not, therefore, fall within the region of equivalence. Let us consider this in the light of a concrete example. One of the experimental questions, already quoted, asked the respondents whether they would prefer a secure job which would never be well-paying, or a well-paying job which would never be secure. In this form of the question, the two goals are stated as incompatible; further, the alternatives were worded in a way to make them as nearly equal in desirability as possible. In this form, then, the alternatives are assumed to fall within the region of equivalence; the set might be represented by the point, A.

The modification is introduced when one alternative is made more desirable than the other. In the present example, there were two such modifications of the original alternatives. The first was one which, so to speak, tipped the scales in favor of selecting the secure job, for it was suggested that this job might someday also become well-paying:

> When we think of the ideal kind of job, most of us would probably agree that we want a secure job which is important and well-paying at the same time. But sometime during their lives many people have to choose between a *secure* job which is not well-paying at the time you take the job but *might* be better paid in the

future, or a well-paying job which would *never* be secure. If you were offered two jobs, *equally interesting and important,* which do you think you would choose?

-- I would choose the *secure* job which was not well-paying at the time but *might* be better paid in the future.
-- I would choose the *well-paying* job which would *never* be secure. (CF, 2)

The preamble to this question was exactly the same as it had been in the original version. The only change is that the wording of one alternative is different. Instead of saying, as we did originally, that selection of the secure job would mean choosing low pay, the new wording suggested that the secure job might possibly someday become a well-paying one. Thus, since the second alternative was unchanged, this modified one becomes relatively the more attractive. In terms of our scheme, this new set of alternatives can be represented by the point, B, in which the first alternative is more desirable than it was in case A but the second alternative is unaffected.

The second modification of the original question was designed to tip the scales in exactly the opposite direction - it was worded in a way which it was hoped would make the well-paying job the more attractive alternative:

When we think of the ideal kind of job, most of us would probably agree that we want a secure job which is important and well-paying at the same time. But sometime during their lives people have to choose between a secure job which would *never* be well-paying, or a *well-paying* job which was not secure at the time you took it but *might* become secure in the future. If you were offered two jobs, *equally interesting and important,* which do you think you would choose?

-- I would choose the *secure* job even though it will *never* be well-paying.

-- I would choose the *well-paying* job, which was not secure at the time that I took it but *might* become secure in the future. (BE, 2)

Here again the preamble remains unchanged, and only the wording of one alternative, in this case the second one, is modified. Locating this set once more in our scheme, it might be represented by the point, C.

This procedure of varying the relative desirability of alternatives was carried out for 15 of the 18 decision problems in our schedule; usually each question was stated in three forms - the "original" version and two modifications.[16] This introduced a problem which has only been alluded to so far. It did not seem reasonable to ask the same respondents to answer all three versions of each question. In the first place this would have made the schedule intolerably long. But perhaps more important was the possibility that respondents would somehow become aware of the purpose of the study, and distort the results in some way. Since the same respondents could not be asked all three forms of the questions, it was necessary to obtain three groups each of which would be asked to answer a different version. It was necessary, furthermore, to find three groups which were similar in all respects: the only possible difference between them was that they were to receive schedules containing slightly different questions. In order to meet these requirements we selected as our subjects students registered in large multi-section courses. This made it possible to distribute each of the schedules to a third of each course. Those participating in one section of a course were assumed to resemble students registered for other sections of the same course; this assumption seems to be justified by the findings.[17]

The same technique of varying the relative strength of alternatives and then studying the consequences of this variation also characterizes experiments in sensory discriminations. Usually the experimenter starts out by presenting two alternatives - let us say weights - which are quite obviously different and therefore relatively easy to discriminate. As the experiment proceeds, the differences between the alternatives are made progressively smaller until they are exactly equal.

There is one major difference between these psycho-physical experiments and those carried out in order to study the phenomenon of unstable questionnaire responses; this leads to a third point in our consideration of how decision dilemmas can be modified experimentally.

(3) *Predispositions and their relation to decision dilemmas:* Psycho-physical experiments deal with discriminations between stimuli which are objectively measurable - in grams, centimeters, or wave lengths. It is therefore possible to know exactly when one stimulus has the same strength as another, when, in other words, the set of alternatives is within the region of equivalence.

Furthermore, the objective difference between the stimuli is the same for all individuals participating in the experiment. If one weight is 24 grams and another is 23 grams, there is a difference of 1 gram between them, regardless of the attitude or personality structure of the subject. True, some individuals may be more sensitive than others to small differences between the stimuli. We should expect, for example, that a musician would be able to distinguish better than non-musicians between two notes which differ only by a quarter-tone. But despite such variations in the ability to discriminate between stimuli, the fact that there is a quarter-tone difference between two notes can be measured objectively and is true for all individuals hearing the notes.

Such is not the case with the relative desirability of goals or the relative effectiveness of alternative policies of action. Although techniques of attitude measurement have progressed considerably over the last decades, they are still not sufficiently precise to indicate that two goals are equally desirable in the same sense that a delicate scale can indicate that two objects weigh the same amount.

Perhaps more serious than this, however, is the fact that there are individual variations in perceiving the relative desirability of two alternative goals. One individual may consider two goals as equally desirable while, for one reason or another, a second individual considers the same two goals very different in their relative desirability. In order to illustrate this possibility, let us return to the example of "secure versus well-paying job," discussed in some detail previously. It was assumed that the original version of the question, in which the two goals were stated as incompatible, would result in the most severe decision dilemma. Some readers may disagree with this contention.

It is possible that, because of particular attitudes, wants or needs, some individuals will *perceive* a particular set of alternatives as equally compelling when, from a detached and "objective" standpoint, they seem quite different in degree of desirability. In other words, it is conceivable that the region of equivalence will be differently located for individuals with various predispositions. Consider, for example, the individual who is especially concerned with security but not with high pay. Will he experience much difficulty in answering the original version of the question? It is unlikely; his special attitudes predispose him to say, without much hesitation, that he would prefer the secure job even though it would never pay well. Pursuing these speculations, we expect that the question form which would give him most difficulty is that in which the alternative satisfying his primary goal is made considerably less attractive than the one satisfying the goal which is only of minor importance to him. In terms of the diagram, we expect that his perceived region of equivalence would move upward to enclose point C.

Persons with opposite predispositions can be expected to behave in exactly opposite fashion. Those who are especially concerned with high pay but not with security will probably not experience much difficulty in deciding between the alternatives of the original question. Nor will they be in a dilemma when faced with a choice between a well-paying job which might become secure, on the one hand, and a secure job which will never be well-paying; the first alternative will, in all probability, seem very much more attractive to them. Their difficulties will arise only when they are asked to choose between alternatives in which the secure job seems to be more attractive. In other words, the region of equivalence for this group of individuals is probably lower than it was in the original diagram, enclosing the point B now.

Considerations such as these indicate the difficulties of talking about the objective difference between two alternatives in the same way that a psycho-physicist can. The set of alternatives which is in the region of equivalence for one group of individuals, with specified needs and interests, will not necessarily be the set in that region for a second group, with different needs and interests. There is probably no set of alternatives which is balanced in strength for *all* individuals; at best we can say that the alternatives are equivalent for *most* people in the sample.

These considerations suggest a pertinent type of analysis. On the basis of collateral information about the respondents, those with different patterns of needs and interests will be distinguished. Once these groups have been separated we shall try to determine whether or not predispositions are reflected in the stability of their responses.

This collateral information can take several forms. First of all, inferences about the respondents' predispositions can be based on their answers to related "index" questions. Three such questions were asked in connection with the job choice:

> How much have you thought about the problem of finding a job when you leave college?
>
> -- A great deal of thought
>
> -- Quite a bit of thought
>
> -- Not much thought
>
> -- No thought at all (A-F,20)
>
> Do you feel that, compared to the average person, you are more likely or less likely to take chances on things which seem good bets?
>
> -- More likely
>
> -- Less likely (A-F,21)
>
> Suppose that you will be married ten years from now. What is the minimum income you would be satisfied with for your family (assuming that there isn't any change in the general scale of salaries)?
>
> $______________ per year (A-F,22)

The first of these questions was intended as a measure of general concern with problems of job-getting; the second was designed to find out, in indirect fashion, the importance attached to security; the final one was meant to provide data concerning desires for high pay. These questions permit us to distinguish groups of respondents with different patterns of interests and concerns; on the basis of these patterns we can predict which groups will find the alternatives equally attractive.

Answers to related index questions furnish a relatively direct means of inferring predispositions. The same kind of inferences can also be based on what might be considered more "remote" data, namely, the demographic characteristics of the respondent. It is generally acknowledged that attitudes and predispositions are molded by the particular social roles of the individual; this knowledge can be used when inferring which respondents will find the offered alternatives equally attractive. We predict, for example, that young girls will be more likely than older girls to find the following alternatives equivalent:

> A girl wants to marry her childhood sweetheart, even though her parents, who have always been very liberal with her, advise her against it. The girl has tried to persuade her parents to see her point of view, but they maintain their attitude. What do you think the girl should do?
>
> -- Follow the advice of her parents
>
> -- Marry her childhood sweetheart against the advice of her parents. (AD, 9)

Young girls are more likely than older ones to depend on their parents. This makes it unlikely that young girls will act counter to their parents' wishes. At the same time, however, girls, both young and old, are apt to find the idea of marrying one's childhood sweetheart particularly romantic; accordingly, they would feel, we expect, that the second alternative is hard to deny. For these reasons, older girls may have few problems in answering the question: the second alternative will probably seem to them so much more compelling than the first that they choose it without difficulty. But it may very well be that younger girls, more dependent on their parents while at the same time believing in romantic love, will feel that neither choice is clearly more attractive than the other.[18]

To summarize the discussion thusfar, our experimental questions can differ in the *types* of decision dilemma which are created; they can differ in the *severity* of the dilemma; they can differ in their relevance for persons with varying predispositions. As yet, however, there has been no indication of how to gauge whether the alternatives in one set are equally desirable, or which of several sets offers alternatives which are most nearly equal in desirability. This is the final point to be considered here.

(4) *Gauging the equivalence of alternatives:* There seem to be two primary techniques for arriving at judgments regarding the equivalence of alternatives. First of all, we can rely on *expert opinion,* asking a number of judges to indicate which of two alternatives is, in their belief, more desirable. This, in a sense, is the technique used by L.L. Thurstone in the development of his attitude scales.[19] In the present study, judgments were not based on the consensus (or averaging) of numerous expert opinions, but rather on the agreement reached by three persons.[20]

In making these ratings we tried to keep in mind the probable attitudes and values of the persons who were to serve as experimental subjects. That is, we did not try to introspect to determine which alternative *we* would find more desirable. Instead, we attempted to put ourselves in the position of the potential subjects and asked, given this kind of attitude, which of these alternatives is more attractive.

The second principal method of determining the equivalence of two alternatives rests on the *symmetry* of the marginal distribution. This procedure is based on the assumption that when two alternatives are considered equally attractive by individuals they will be chosen with equal frequency by a group; and, conversely, when one of the alternatives is very much more attractive than the other, that alternative will be chosen considerably more frequently. Relatively symmetrical marginals will therefore be taken as indicative of relatively equivalent alternatives; relatively skewed marginals as evidence of unequal attractiveness of the two alternatives.[21]

By and large both methods of judging equivalence lead to the same conclusions. This can be seen in Table 5 which makes use, once more, of the question asking for a choice between a secure and a well-paying job:

Table 5

The set of alternatives considered most nearly equivalent has the most symmetrical marginal distribution.

Opinion Regarding Relative Attractiveness of the Alternatives	Percent Who Choose the "Secure" Job		
	Interview I	Interview II	Total Cases
The two are equally attractive	46	47	179
"Well-paying" is more attractive	21	20	181
"Secure" is more attractive	79	76	189

There are two features of special interest in Table 5. First of all, the great constancy of the marginal distributions should be noted. On all three of the schedules, the number of students choosing the secure job was virtually the same in both interviews.

But the second point, and the one of greater interest at the moment, is that common-sense expectations regarding the relative attractiveness of the different alternatives is very clearly reflected in the marginals. When the two alternatives were set up as being equally attractive, as they were in the original form of the question, they were selected with almost equal frequency; the marginal distribtion was only slightly asymmetrical. In the second version of the question, where the well-paying job was made the more attractive one, the number of respondents choosing the secure job decreased markedly. Similarly, in the final version of the question, where the secure job was made the more attractive alternative, the number of students selecting it increased markedly. Most importantly, the marginal distributions were noticeably asymmetrical in the two modified versions.

In some instances expectations regarding the equivalence of different alternatives were not correct in the light of other evidence. While it does not bear directly on the central problem, it is worthwhile to digress for a moment to consider the implications of these errors. For example, one question presented a choice problem familiar and meaningful to all students, namely, the choice between studying and enjoying oneself. We assumed that all of the subjects would consider "having fun" a highly desirable goal. The problem was then to call for a choice between the prospect of fun and work of varying degrees of urgency. In its original form the question read:

> Suppose that you had planned to stay home one particular evening to work on a difficult term paper due a week later. In the late afternoon you learn that two very good friends of yours have announced their engagement and that there will be a big party for them that evening. What do you think you probably would do?
>
> -- Stay home and work on the paper
>
> -- Go to the party (CF, 12)

By specifying that the required work was a difficult term paper we hoped to suggest that it was something which called for considerable preparation; by indicating that it was due in one week's time we hoped to suggest that the loss of an evening, originally planned for this work, would make it hard to meet the deadline. This, it was thought, would create a serious dilemma for the students.

Both modifications sought to lessen this dilemma. In both of the modified versions the prospect of going to a party was held constant; the seriousness and imminence of the work requirement was varied. Thus in one modification the school assignment was made *less* urgent than it had been in the original statement of the question:

> Suppose that you had planned to stay home one particular evening to catch up on past reading assignments...
>
> -- Stay home and read
>
> -- Go to the party (AD, 12)

Catching up on reading assignments is something which can be fitted into one's schedule more easily than a term paper; it is not the kind of work which requires immediate or urgent attention. It was assumed, therefore, that the decision called for in this question would be less difficult than it was in the original form.

The second modification attempted to made the school assignment *more* urgent than it had been originally:

> Suppose that you had planned to stay home one particular evening to study for a tough final examination to be given the following day...
>
> -- Stay home and study
>
> -- Go to the party (BE, 12)

A tough final examination to be taken the next day seemed to us so urgent an assignment that we expected the subjects to experience little difficulty in making the decision between staying home to study and going to a party.

The original version of the question, it was expected, would show a nearly symmetrical distribution of choices, and each of the modifications asymmetrical distributions. We expected that, let us say, 30 percent of the respondents would choose to read assignments rather than go to a party and, conversely, that 70 percent would choose to study for a final examination instead of going to a party. The extent to which these expectations were incorrect is shown in Table 6.

Table 6

The set of alternatives considered most nearly equivalent does *not* have the most symmetrical distribution

	Set of Alternatives		
	Read vs. party	Write paper vs. party	Study for final exam vs. party
Study	8%	20%	52%
Go to party	92	80	48
Total	179	180	190

Apparently the attraction of a party had been underestimated. Reference to the type of scheme first introduced on page 34 will help summarize both the expectations and the actual findings of our study.

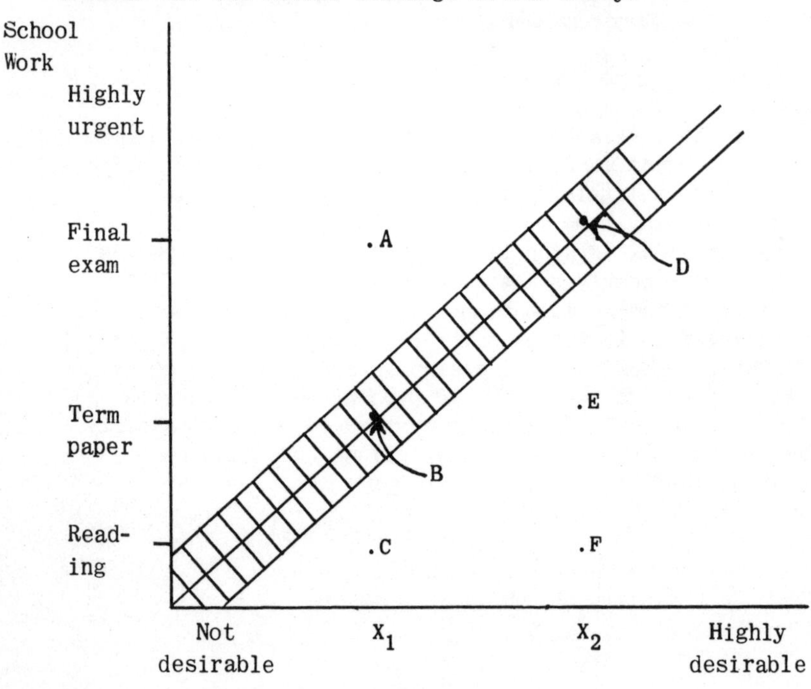

There can be little doubt that a final examination is a more urgent assignment than a term paper due sometime in the future; there can be little doubt that a term paper is a more urgent assignment than reading for one's courses. It is fairly certain, therefore, that the alternatives have been located correctly on the vertical axis. The mistake was apparently made in locating the alternative on the horizontal axis. We assumed that it was at X_1. Had it been, the original expectations would have been fulfilled. The choice between staying home to work on a term paper or going to a party would have been in the region of equivalence (B) and would, therefore, have presented most difficulties; the other sets of alternatives, one above (A) and one below (C) that region, would have been less difficult. The results suggest, however, that the alternative of going to a party is more attractive than assumed originally; apparently it is located at point X_2 (relatively speaking) instead of at X_1. Only through that location can the results be understood. It seems likely, then, that the prospect of going to a party is so attractive for college students that only when faced with a final examination on the next day do they consider not going.[22]

In this instance the two methods of judging equivalence did not agree. There were other cases in which it was not entirely clear just what to expect. In both of these situations symmetry of the marginals will be relied on to indicate which set of alternatives is most nearly equivalent.

According to our original proposition, the more nearly equivalent the alternatives, the more difficulty the subject will experience in choosing between them. The meaning of equivalence has been outlined in some detail. We have seen how dilemmas can be experimentally modified and how their presence can be determined. What remains is a discussion of how to detect whether or not subjects experienced difficulties in making the decisions required of them.

Detection of Difficulties

Verbal reports are perhaps the most direct way in which the respondent can express his difficulties. In order to make sure that such expressions would be obtained systematically from all respondents, rather than being offered haphazardly, a special "difficulty question" was asked in conjunction with each of the decision questions. The form which this question took, and accompanying instructions to the respondents, were as follows:

> You may feel that some of the questions are difficult to answer because they ask you to make hard decisions. *Answer each one to the best of your ability.*
>
> We would like to know, however, just how difficult each question was for you. Therefore, in the right-hand margin of the page you will find a place to indicate the degree of difficulty you had. *Please be sure to check the appropriate box after answering each question.* If you want to comment further on your reactions to the questions, do so in the blank spaces in the right-hand margin.
>
> Difficulty
> answering:
>
> -- Great
>
> -- Some
>
> -- Little

These reported difficulties will be basic to much of the analysis.

Respondents can also express their difficulties in certain forms of *behavior.* One of these is the *length of time* that it takes to choose between the alternatives. Assuming that the subject has no difficulty in understanding the task required of him, it is likely that the longer he takes to respond, the more difficulty he has experienced in making a choice. Because the decision is not immediately obvious to him, because he has to weigh the relative merits of the different alternatives, it takes him some time to arrive at a final, although perhaps temporary, answer. A second manifestation is one of *vacillation back and forth* between the alternatives. The actual form which this vacillation takes depends on the interview situation. If the interview is conducted as a personal one, the vacillation will consist in the respondent's selection of one alternative and then correction to select another. The same kind of vacillation will be observed in erasures made by the respondent when the interview is self-administered in the form of a paper-and-pencil test. Still another behavioral manifestation of experienced difficulties is found in the respondent's *refusal to answer* a question. While such refusals probably have a number of different sources, one of them is undoubtedly the fact that the respondent finds the difficulty of deciding between the alternatives too great and therefore does not even want to make the decision. Closely related to this indication of difficulty is a fourth one, namely the *insistence on giving qualified answers*. One way in which the respondent escapes the dilemma in which the question places him is to add to his answer - his selection of one alternative - enough qualifications so that the dilemma no longer exists.

Most of these manifestations can be directly observed only in a face-to-face situation. That is, we cannot very well ask the respondent to tell us how long he took to answer the question; whether his failure to respond to one item represented a refusal rather than negligence; and so on. For this information we must rely on the interviewer or other observer.

The subjects in the present experiment were interviewed neither individually nor personally. Instead, they were given self-administered paper-and-pencil tests in large groups. As a result none of these behavioral manifestations of difficulty is available. When we talk of the difficulties experienced by our respondents, we shall mean those reported by them in answer to the corollary question.

The fairly complicated hypothesis being studied here and the rather intricate procedure proposed for testing it have required us to spend considerable time merely clarifying the variables. With this discussion completed, the actual results can be reported in brief and concise form.[23]

Equivalence of the Alternatives and Difficulty of the Choice

Before studying how these factors are related to instability of response, it is necessary to establish that there is, in fact, a relationship between equivalence of the alternatives and degree of difficulty in selecting one. Is it true that when alternatives are equally attractive, by some criterion, respondents experience special difficulty in deciding between them?

Usually, we recall, three sets of alternatives were presented for each choice problem. Do those respondents faced with the most nearly equivalent set experience the most severe dilemma? Table 7 shows the answer for the job question:

Table 7

Respondents asked to select between nearly equivalent alternatives experience more of a dilemma than do those choosing between alternatives differing in their relative attractiveness

Relative Attractiveness of the Alternatives	Percent Reporting "Little" Difficulty in Both Interviews[24]
The two are equally attractive	37
"Well-paying" is more attractive	52
"Secure" is more attractive	59

Only slightly more than a third of those asked to choose between the nearly equivalent alternatives could claim in both interviews that they had experienced little difficulty in answering; over half of those asked the modified versions of the question reported that they had no trouble either time in selecting an answer.

In an earlier table (see Table 5 above) the marginal distribution of each version of the job question was studied. That information, when taken in conjunction with the proportion of respondents reporting little difficulty, makes it possible to study the correspondence between the symmetry and the associated difficulty of each set of alternatives. For example, the marginal distribution of the set of equally attractive alternatives was more symmetrical than the marginals of either of the modified versions. At the same time, greater difficulty was associated with these equally attractive alternatives than with the others. Thus, the set of alternatives which ranks first in symmetry also ranks first in difficulty. But the correspondence is not complete. The set of alternatives which has the lowest degree of symmetry - that in which the "well-paying" job is more attractive - was not considered easiest to choose between; more persons reported difficulties in answering this set than in answering the other modified version of the question. We shall therefore say that this question has one degree of deviation from complete correspondence between amount of symmetry and level of difficulty. This notion of deviation from correspondence needs clarification.

In general, there are four different possibilities. There are, first of all, cases of complete correspondence, where each set of alternatives has the same ranking on both variables. An example of this is Question 4 on the conflict schedule.[25] The version of this question which has the most symmetrical marginals is also most difficult to answer; the version which is intermediate in symmetry is also intermediate in difficulty; and the version which is most asymmetrical in marginal distribution is also easiest to answer. Secondly, there are cases of complete *lack* of correspondence. An example of this is Question 14. In this instance, the set of alternatives with the most symmetrical marginals is the one in connection with which least difficulties were reported; while the alternatives which were most asymmetrical in their marginal distribution were considered most difficult to choose between. The remaining two possibilities are characterized by neither complete correspondence nor by complete lack of it. In some cases, like the job question to which we have referred at numerous points, there is one deviation from complete correspondence. This can come about in either of two ways: when the sets of alternatives rank 1, 2, 3 on the one variable and 1, 3, 2 on the other; or when they rank 1, 2, 3 on the one variable and 2, 1, 3 on the other.[26] In still other instances, there may be two deviations of this kind. This situation also can come about in either of two ways, represented by the two patterns (1,2,3; 2,3,1) or (1,2,3; 3,1,2).

Our hypothesis about the relationship between symmetry and difficulty will be confirmed to the extent that the questions show such correspondence. But, as is usual in analyses of this kind, we must test our findings against chance expectations. The reader can easily verify for himself that, out of a total of 12 questions,[27] two can be expected to show complete correspondence by chance alone, four will show one deviation, an additional four will show two deviations, and the remaining two will exhibit complete lack of correspondence. Reference to the actual findings indicates that the observed patterns are not likely to have come about by chance alone.

Table 8

There are few and slight deviations from the expected pattern that the set of alternatives with most symmetrical marginals is most difficult to answer and the set of alternatives with least symmetrical marginals easiest to answer.

Deviations from pattern of complete correspondence	Number of questions
0	5
1	5
2	1
3	1
Total questions	12

When a Chi-square test is applied to this distribution, it develops that there are only about 5 chances in 100 that such a distribution could arise through chance alone. This we take as fairly positive evidence that there is indeed a negative relationship between symmetry of the marginals, denoting equal attractiveness of the alternatives, and ease of making a choice between the alternative.

Equivalence of the Alternatives and Instability of Response

In studying the relationship between equivalence of the alternatives and experienced difficulties, we have examined the way in which the independent variable is related to the intervening factor. We are now in a position to determine the extent to which each of these factors is related to the dependent phenomenon - instability of response.

Starting first with equivalence of the alternatives, there is evidence of a fairly close relationship. In Table 9 the job question is called on once more to illustrate the procedure used in this analysis. First of all, the turnover index has been calculated for groups answering the different sets of alternatives:

Table 9

Those presented with the set of most nearly equivalent alternatives are slightly less stable in their choices than are those presented with alternatives differing more in relative attractiveness.

Relative Attractiveness of the Alternatives	Index Value	Number of Cases
The two are equally attractive	.06	179
"Well-paying" is more attractive	.04	181
"Secure" is more attractive	.03	189

While the index value is slightly larger when the two alternatives are stated as being equally attractive, the differences are by no means large in this case.

The second step is to relate the turnover index to the symmetry of the marginals, making use of a mode of analysis which is similar to that employed in the previous section. Here a positive relationship is expected. That is, it is our hypothesis that, as the symmetry of the marginals increases so will the instability of response, as measured by the turnover index.

In the job question, there is one deviation from complete correspondence, for the set of alternatives which has the most asymmetrical marginal distribution, the second one, has slightly higher turnover than the set of medium symmetry, the last. The total picture, however, shows an even closer relationship than was observed between equivalence and difficulty:

Table 10

There are few and slight deviations from the expected pattern that the set of alternatives with most symmetrical marginals receives most unstable answers and the set of alternatives with least symmetrical marginals receives most stable answers.

Deviations from pattern of complete correspondence	Number of questions
0	6
1	8
2	1
3	-
Total questions	15

It was possible to carry out this analysis for 15 of the 18 choice problems. When a Chi-square test is applied to these data,[28] it turns out that there is less than one chance in 100 that such a distribution could come about by chance alone.

Difficulty of the Choice and Instability of Response

The final relationship to be explored is that between experienced difficulties and the dependent variable, turnover of response. The question to be raised here is whether those who report difficulties make less stable choices than those reporting no trouble.

Up to this point in the analysis the unit of investigation has been particular sets of alternatives. We have studied whether, among several sets of related alternatives, that one with the most equivalent alternatives results in the most unstable responses; or whether the same set is most often reported as posing difficulties of decision.

Now individual respondents can be made the unit of our analysis. They can be classified according to the amount of difficulty which they report having experienced, and can then be examined to see whether those reporting greater difficulties give more unstable answers. Table 11 does exactly this, making use once more of the perhaps overworked job question:

Table 11

Those who reported difficulty in choosing between a secure or a well-paying job (in the original version of the question) are less stable in their responses.

Reported Difficulties:	Index Value	Number of Cases [29]
Some or great	.07	64
Little	.03	64

Comparable analysis of the other sets of alternatives reveals exactly the same result for most of the cases. As Table 12 indicates, those who experienced some or great difficulty are almost invariably less stable in their choice of alternatives than are those who experienced little difficulty.[30] While in 5 cases the respondents who experienced a dilemma revealed as much stability as those reporting no such experience, in *no* case did they show a greater degree of consistency. In other words, while our expectation was not always confirmed, it was never refuted.

The three relationships which have been investigated in these sections can be related to each other in the following way:

Equivalence ⟶ Experienced Difficulties ⟶ Stability

There is a fourth type of relationship which might be explored: that between equivalence and stability for groups reporting different degrees of difficulty. If experienced difficulties really do interpret the relationship between equivalence and stability, then these "partial relationships," as they are called, should vanish.[31] We were unable to carry out this kind of analysis in any systematic fashion, because there were not enough cases. Tentatively,

Table 12

In most questions those who report some or great difficulty are less stable in their responses than those reporting little difficulty.

	Number of Questions
Respondents reporting some or great difficulty show *less* stability than do those reporting little difficulty	32
Respondents reporting some or great difficulty show *as much* stability as do those reporting little difficulty	5
Respondents reporting some or great difficulty show *more* stability than do those reporting little difficulty	-
Total questions	37

however, it appears that the relationship between equivalence and stability does indeed decrease when experienced difficulties are introduced as the intervening variable.

Predispositions, Equivalence of Alternatives and Instability of Response

In an earlier section (see pp. 38-42 above) it was suggested that respondents with different constellations of needs and interests would be predisposed to find certain alternatives more similar in relative attractiveness than would subjects with other attitudes and concerns. So far, however, these predispositions have not been taken into account.

While it would be too space consuming to report this kind of analysis for all of the decision problems,[32] the results are generally of enough substantive interest to warrant discussion of one example. One question, we recall, asked the respondents whether they believed a girl should marry her childhood sweetheart even though her parents disapproved, or whether she should follow the advice of her father and mother. The hypothesis set forth earlier was that young girls would be more likely than older ones to find these two alternatives of the same relative attractiveness. Our reasoning was that, while both young and older girls would find the idea of marrying a childhood sweetheart romantic and therefore desirable, young girls are at the same time more dependent on their parents and therefore less likely to disregard their advice.

These speculations lead us to look for certain specific findings.[33] First of all, it is necessary to check the assumption that dependence on one's family is a function of age. One of the index questions included in our schedule asked:

> Compared to other students you know, would you say that you feel closer to your parents, not as close, or about as close?
>
> -- Closer to my parents
>
> -- Not as close to my parents
>
> -- About as close to my parents (A-F, 19)

Table 13 shows that a feeling of closeness to one's parents does indeed vary with the age of the girl:

Table 13

Younger girls more often report feeling closer to their parents than other students whom they know.

	Girls Under 21	Girls 21 and Over
Feel closer	54%	44%
About as close	30	33
Not as close	16	23
Total cases	117	43

A second question concerns the relative attractiveness of the alternatives in the two age groups. Do the younger girls find the two possible choices relatively more equivalent than is the case among older women students? The answer is an affirmative one; Table 14 shows that the marginal split is more symmetrical for the younger girls:

Table 14

The marginal distribution is more symmetrical for the younger as compared with the older girls.

	Percent Saying the Girl Should "Follow the Advice of Her Parents"		
	Interview I	Interview II	Number of Cases
Girls under 21	23	27	117
Girls 21 and over	12	14	42

While in neither case can the distribution be considered symmetrical, it is relatively more so for the younger girls. And, as was to be expected, the younger girls show their greater dependence on their parents by indicating more frequently that the girl about whom they are questioned should follow the advice of her mother and father.

These two findings suggest that the alternatives are closer to the region of equivalence for the young girls. Do we find, in consequence, that they experience greater difficulties? The answer is again affirmative: 60 percent of the older, as compared with 34 percent of the younger, reported in both interviews that they had little difficulty in answering the question.

All of these findings lead to the expectation that stability of response will also be a function of age. This too is the case, as Table 15 shows:

Table 15

Younger girls give less stable answers than older when asked whether or not someone should follow the advice of his parents.

	Index Value	Number of Cases
Girls under 21	.05	117
Girls 21 and over	.00	42

In summary, by considering certain predispositions we were able to predict which respondents would experience the alternatives as relatively more equivalent and which, therefore, would make less stable choices.

This series of findings rounds out the main analysis of the materials. There are two further findings, however, of sufficient interest to receive special attention. One of these deals with the stability of cognitive discriminations; the second deals with cases in which the respondents themselves tell us how closely balanced two alternatives are.

The Stability of Cognitive Discriminations

One type of decision dilemma, already mentioned in an earlier section, is that which arises when respondents are asked to distinguish between statements very alike in meaning, in truth, and so on. These *cognitive dilemmas*, as they might be called, are probably the closest parallel in survey research to the type of situation set up by psychophysicists. Do they follow the same pattern observed in connection with goal dilemmas?

There were three questions of this kind in our schedule. Each of these was asked in three versions, which modified the similarity of the alternatives.

(1) *Size of the Army:* The first of these questions asked how many men had served in the Army at the height of its strength during World War II. The different sets of alternatives were: 7,000,000 or 3,000,000 (AD,29); 7,000,000 or 25,000,000 (BE,29); and 7,000,000 or 6,000,000 (CF,29). It is our expectation that this last set of alternatives, with objectively the smallest difference, will pose the greatest dilemma. It is difficult to know which of the other sets will create the least serious problem; we shall not attempt any guess.

Respondents were not asked to report the difficulties they experienced in answering these different sets of alternatives. But the symmetry of the marginal distributions can be studied and then related to instability of the discrimination. Let us start by considering the equivalence of the alternatives as this is revealed in symmetry of the marginals:

Table 16

The set of alternatives with the smallest objective difference has the highest degree of symmetry.

At the height of the war the Army had 7,000,000 or	Percent Saying "7,000,000"		
	Interview I	Interview II	Number of Cases
6,000,000 men	69	64	179
25,000,000 men	70	72	174
3,000,000 men	85	84	171

In this particular instance the differences in symmetry are only very slight. Nonetheless they are in the right direction; the set of alternatives which we expected would create the greatest difficulty in discrimination has a somewhat more symmetrical distribution of answers.

The greater difficulty of choosing between very similar alternatives is revealed in the frequency with which the respondents wavered between the two answers:

Table 17

The set of alternatives with the smallest objective differences has the highest degree of turnover.

At the height of the war, the Army had 7,000,000 or	Index Value	Number of Cases
6,000,000	.15	179
25,000,000	.06	174
3,000,000	.08	171

First of all, note that amount of instability runs parallel to degree of symmetry; this we expect from our previous analysis of goal dilemmas. But a second, perhaps unexpected, feature of Table 17 is the high index value for the first set of alternatives. Apparently there is even more vacillation in connection with cognitive dilemmas of this kind than there was when individuals had to choose between alternative goals.

(2) *Date of Battle of Gettysburg:* The second problem in cognitive discrimination dealt with another kind of fact - the exact date of the Battle of Gettysburg. Again there were three sets of alternatives: July, 1863 or September, 1863 (AD,30); 1863 or 1864 (BE,30); and, finally, 1812 or 1863 (CF,30). The marginal distributions indicate the difficulty experienced in selecting either alternative of the first two sets:

Table 18

The sets of alternatives which are most alike have the highest degree of symmetry.

	Percent Giving Correct Answer		
	Interview I	Interview II	Number of Cases
July, 1863, or Sept., 1863	55	60	167
1863 or 1864	53	57	167
1863 or 1812	85	90	185

From the marginal distributions, we would guess that the first two sets of alternatives are perceived as being almost equally difficult. The skewness of marginals in the final set may be taken as evidence of the greater ease of choosing between those alternatives.[34]

The symmetry of the first two sets suggests, further, that subjects will waver between the alternatives, that they will, in other words, give unstable responses. The greater ease of choice in the final set should be reflected in greater stability. This indeed is the case:

Table 19

The sets of alternatives which are most alike have the highest degree of turnover.

	Index Value	Number of Cases
July, 1863, or Sept., 1863	.22	167
1863 or 1864	.14	167
1863 or 1812	.02	185

The first two sets have significantly higher turnover than the third. And, although it was not reflected in the symmetry of marginals, the first set, that with the objectively smallest difference, was answered with least consistency.

(3) *Title of Darwin's work:* The final problem in cognitive discrimination concerned the exact title of Darwin's most famous work. As in the previous cases, three sets of alternatives, of varying similarity, were presented: "The Origin of Species" or "The Origin of the Species" (BE,36); "The Origin of Species" or "The Meaning of Relativity" (AD,36); and "The Origin of Species" or "Up From the Apes" (CF,36).

The first set of alternatives contains only a minor and hairsplitting distinction. In line with our hypothesis, therefore, it was expected that those presented with this set would experience most difficulty in making the required discrimination, and would be least stable in the discriminations which they finally did make. Again these expectations are borne out, both in the frequency with which the correct answer is given and in the examination of turnover.

While few subjects thought that Darwin's work was entitled "The Meaning of Relativity" or "Up From the Apes", about half believed that it was called "The Origin of *the* Species:"

Table 20

The set of alternatives with the smallest objective difference has the highest degree of symmetry.

The correct title of Darwin's work is "The Origin of Species" or	Percent Saying "The Origin of Species"		
	Interview I	Interview II	No. of Cases
"The Origin of the Species"	47	55	170
"The Meaning of Relativity"	90	91	168
"Up From the Apes"	92	91	173

In previous examples of cognitive dilemmas, it was not always possible to say that the set of alternatives considered most alike objectively was at the same time the most symmetrical in marginal distribution. Here, however, there is no problem.[35]

The equivalence of the alternatives is reflected, furthermore, in the instability of those required to choose between them:

Table 21

The set of alternatives with the smallest objective differences has the highest degree of turnover.

The correct title of Darwin's work is "The Origin of Species" or	Index Value	Number of Cases
"The Origin of the Species"	.11	170
"The Meaning of Relativity"	.05	168
"Up From the Apes"	.03	173

In summary, subjects seem to respond to cognitive dilemmas just as they did to goal dilemmas. When the distinctions are minor ones, the two alternatives are selected with more or less equal frequency. At the same time, however, there is considerable vacillation from one alternative to the other.

Expressions of Equivalence and Instability of Response

In all of the choice problems considered thusfar, we have relied on expert opinion, on marginal symmetry, or on inferences from predispositions to indicate whether two alternatives are equivalent in their attractiveness. By and large, these inferences led to expected results. Nonetheless, it seemed desirable to provide one opportunity in which respondents themselves could indicate the relative equivalence of any two alternatives. Further, we wanted to see whether, when equivalence is established in this way, it bears the same relationship to stability of response as it did when it was inferred by methods outlined above.

The opportunity to express the equivalence of alternatives was provided by asking all of our respondents to rank certain qualities:

> We know that a friend generally has many desirable qualities, but we would like to know which in the following list seem *most* important to you. Place a "1" in front of the quality which you consider most important for a friend to have, a "2" beside the next most important quality, and so on for all five in our list.
>
> --Loyalty
>
> --Generosity
>
> --Brilliance
>
> --Sense of humor
>
> --Good appearance
>
> (A-F,10)

Our assumption was that those qualities which were assigned *adjacent* ranks would be most nearly equivalent in perceived importance. That is, those qualities ranked first and second by an individual are more nearly equivalent for him than are those which he ranks first and fifth, let us say.

Data on stability was obtained in the following way. Each of the qualities was paired with every other, resulting in a list of ten combinations. The respondents were then instructed in both interviews:

> We would like you to circle the quality in *each* of the ten pairs which you would be most likely to look for in a friend. (You will draw ten circles in all.)

At the conclusion of the second interview it was possible to determine, for each pair, how many subjects had shifted from one quality to the other.

The question now is whether stability of response is related to equivalence of the alternatives. For example, do those who ranked "loyalty" and "generosity" first and second show less stability than those who ranked them first and fifth.[36] Do those who ranked "good appearance" and "sense of humor" second and fourth manifest more stability than those who rated these qualities second and fifth?

It requires a somewhat complicated analysis to answer these questions. Working separately with each pair of qualities - "loyalty" and "generosity", for example - it was necessary, first, to distinguish between those subjects who considered these two qualities of almost equal importance and those who considered them very different in importance. This was accomplished by referring back to the first part of the question, in which the several qualities had been ranked. By examining the rankings assigned to "loyalty" and to "generosity," respectively, it was possible to isolate those for whom loyalty and generosity differed by one rank, those who, in other words, rated loyalty first and generosity second, or second and third, and so on. It was also possible to isolate those for whom these two qualities differed by two ranks (for example, they were ranked first and third, or second and fourth); and those for whom the same qualities differed by three or four ranks. These procedures furnished three different groups of respondents, one in which the two qualities were perceived as being *almost equal* in attractiveness, a second in which there was *some difference* in relative attractiveness, and a final one in which there was a *great difference* in the relative importance attached to the two qualities.

The second and crucial step in the analysis was to determine the stability of decision between these qualities within each of the three groups. Making use of the second part of the question, where the respondents were asked twice to choose between loyalty and generosity, it was possible to study the turnover in these choices among those for whom the two qualities differed by one rank, among those for whom they differed by two ranks, and among those for whom they differed by three or four ranks.

The same procedures were repeated for the nine other pairs of qualities. Table 22 reports the results for each of the pairs separately, and for all combined. The figures in Table 22 are the values of the familiar turnover index. By and large, the questions which we raised initially find affirmative answers, for qualities which were assigned adjacent

Table 22

Those who believe that the qualities differ in importance by one rank are less stable in their choices than those who believe that the qualities differ more.

	Difference of one rank	Difference of two ranks	Difference of three or four ranks
Loyalty or generosity	.05	.03	.00
Sense of humor or brilliance	.10	.02	.01
Good appearance or loyalty	.02	.04	.03
Brilliance or good appearance	.13	.06	.04
Loyalty or sense of humor	.06	.03	.00
Good appearance or sense of humor	.11	.01	.03
Generosity or brilliance	.10	.06	.02
Loyalty or brilliance	.12	.04	.00
Sense of humor or generosity	.16	.08	.00
Generosity or good appearance	.16	.06	.03
All pairs	.10	.04	.02

rankings generally were selected with less stability than were qualities assigned very different rankings. That is, greater instability is generally associated with greater equivalence of the alternatives. These findings suggest, further, that when equivalence is established by the respondents themselves it bears the same relationship to instability of response as it does when it is established by expert opinion, by inferences from marginal symmetry, or by some other means.

CHAPTER 2

ROLE OF MOOD

In the first chapter we considered one set of factors making for changes in *answers* to the questions asked in panel studies. We presented some evidence to show that, when a respondent has difficulty deciding between two alternatives because of their equal attractiveness to him, he will in all probability waver back and forth from one to the other.

Clearly, though, there will be cases in which a change in response is indicative of a change in attitude or opinion. It is now our task to find pressures bringing about these "real" changes. Characteristics of the phenomenon we are studying immediately tell us much about the nature of these influences. We are concerned essentially with trying to explain how it can happen that the marginal distributions of response remain constant from one interview to the next while there is always some degree of internal variation. The only influences which can operate to produce this phenomenon are those distributed *at random* in the population. Some persons must be exposed to pressures making for more positive attitudes; an almost equal number of persons must be exposed to pressures working in the opposite direction. If this were not the case, the marginals would not remain constant over a period of time. If everyone in the population were subjected to influences leading to a more positive attitude, then the proportions of persons holding the positive attitude would steadily increase.

Some of these pressures are *internal*; that is, their immediate locus is within the individual. Others are *external*; they are events in the outside world and, essentially, everything that is not internal. This distinction is a useful one, as it enables us to organize our observations in a more systematic fashion. But it is a fairly loose one, for, in the last analysis, it is probably possible to trace all internal pressures to external influences. We shall see, however, that in common sense terms at least there does seem to be a difference between the two.

I. ANALYSIS OF EXISTING PANEL MATERIALS

As in the previous chapter, our first clues to the way in which internal and external pressures produce unstable responses came from existing survey materials, and, more especially, from panel studies. In this instance, however, the available data were wholly qualitative in nature. They were, in essence, the accounts given by subjects to explain why they had answered the same questions differently on different occasions.

Mood Changes and Instability of Response

As we acquire greater experience in survey procedures, we recognize the variety of variables which must be taken into account in interpreting our findings. We know that expressions of opinion should be evaluated in the light of different levels of information or interest. In recent years the importance of variables whose relevance was less obvious has been demonstrated. Seasonal variations in opinion on various issues, for example, require the analyst to take into account the time of year at which his questions are asked.

There is another variable of this kind - the *mood* of the respondent at the time that he is questioned - which has not received the attention which it perhaps deserves. In every survey we assume, implicitly, that our subjects are not in an abnormal state of mind at the time that we interview them; we also assume, again implicitly, that the mood of one respondent is similar to that of another. But these are patently unrealistic assumptions. We know, from our own experience, that we undergo periodic changes in mood. We also know that this may well affect the way in which we answer a questionnaire; mood changes act as internal pressures. When we are in a particularly good mood, for whatever reason, we are probably more optimistic about the future than we would be otherwise; we may be more friendly toward persons and groups; we may be more voluble in our discussion. When, on the other hand, we find ourselves in a particularly bad mood, then optimism gives way to pessimism, friendliness to aggression, and volubility to curtness.

While it might be said that the respondent's mood is of importance in any kind of survey, it becomes apparent only in panel studies. For some of the shifts in answers which we observe seem to result from changes in mood. Thus, in one of the intensive interviews from the Baltimore Study we read the following:

> (Did you ever agree that it would be a good idea not to hire Jews?) I think I probably said that. It depends on the mood you're in, whether you are thinking of yourself for what there is. *Right now things are not going too badly and I am in a pretty fair frame of mind. Maybe things weren't good last time.*

Or again, a respondent whose expressed attitudes toward the Palestine conflict had shifted, explained his change in the following way:

> I'm in sympathy with the Arabs. (Last time the interviewer wrote down that you didn't want either one of them to win.) *I changed my mind.* (What made you change your mind?) I couldn't tell you that. (Do you talk about it with friends?) I've discussed it, but I can't remember what it's all about. I haven't followed it up. I haven't paid too much attention to it. I can't tell the reason. *Maybe I was in a different mood.*

The implication of this comment, that mood plays a more important role when the attitude is relatively peripheral, suggests a condition for the greater or lesser relevance of this factor. When the issue is of great concern to the respondent, his mood is perhaps less likely to influence his answers. This possibility was stated quite explicitly by one of the more self-analytical subjects in our sample. After disagreeing that "Generally speaking, Negroes are lazy and ignorant," this woman asked the interviewer:

> What did I say about that question; how did I answer it the first time? I agreed with it? I must have been feeling differently that day. (Do you think

> **that your opinions depend on how you feel?)** *No, I don't think that real deep opinions change with how you feel. If the opinion is deep enough, it won't. If it's just a shallow opinion and doesn't mean much, then it might.*

Because existing panel studies do not contain questions which could be used as indicators of mood, it was impossible to find statistical evidence bearing on this point. It was necessary, therefore, to devise a special experiment; the results of this will be reported in the second part of this chapter.

But while the evidence available in existing panel studies is scanty, it suggests that mood is an effective internal pressure bringing about changes in attitude. Moods are not usually spontaneously generated, however; if we could trace them back we would usually find that a bad mood develops as the result of some external event. It therefore becomes appropriate to turn to the external pressures which might account for our phenomenon of constant marginals but internal variation.

Molecular Pressures and Instability of Response

In order to clarify the nature of these external pressures, it might be helpful to distinguish several major types of stimuli. The first and perhaps most obvious are those involved in a question such as: "What is the effect of the war in Korea on attitudes toward universal military training?" or "How does the creation of Israel as an independent state affect attitudes toward Jews?" The stimuli in question here - war in Korea and the creation of Israel - are what might be called *universal* or *mass experiences*. Presumably everyone in the population is exposed to them.

Generally we are interested to see whether these stimuli lead to changes in the marginal distribution of attitudes: does war in Korea lead to greater acceptance of military training; does the creation of Israel make for an improvement in attitudes toward Jews? Questions of this kind do not concern us, for we have limited ourselves to investigating the phenomenon of constant marginals.

It is conceivable, however, that a universal stimulus will fall within the province of our research. If it affects sub-groups of the population differently, it can happen that we find constant marginals with internal variation. One example deals with changes in attitude toward Justice Hugo Black following the disclosure that he had previously been associated with the Ku Klux Klan. The distribution of attitude after that disclosure was found to be very much like what it had been beforehand.[1] Nevertheless there were a considerable number of changers, persons who shifted from a positive to a negative attitude and persons who changed in the opposite direction. The explanation for this was that the disclosure had apparently affected religious sub-groups differently. Prior to the publicity about Black's early associations he had drawn his main support from Catholics and Jews; they responded to the disclosure by becoming negative in attitude. Protestants, on the other hand, who originally had been relatively anti-Black, responded to the disclosure by becoming more favorable in attitude.

Constant marginals usually mean that we are dealing with a different type of stimulus, however. A second variety are those personal, perhaps idiosyncratic, experiences which individuals encounter in their everyday lives. Conversations with friends or relatives, personal contacts with strangers, chance remarks overheard in public - such are the experiences we have in mind here. These *molecular pressures,* as they might be called, are often not duplicated for any other individual; if they are duplicated, it is *at random* within the population.

Again, existing panel studies provide only qualitative data regarding the effectiveness of molecular pressures.[2] Let us consider the nature of this evidence. We shall focus on the attitudes which a group of white individuals hold toward Negroes. During the course of several weeks time some of these individuals undoubtedly have experiences which make their attitudes toward Negroes less favorable. Other persons, however, will certainly experience situations or events which produce more favorable attitudes. In other words, since the events and experiences are randomly distributed, their net effect is to cancel each other out. Thus, while a number of persons undergo changes in attitude, the overall feeling toward Negroes remains the same.

Since these molecular pressures are individual (even idiosyncratic) experiences, it is, by definition, virtually impossible to find any statistical evidence of their operation. When, however, we intensively interview subjects who have given different answers to repeated questions, we sometimes find that these shifting answers seem to reflect a change in attitude in response to personal stimuli.

The intensive interviews with members of the Baltimore panel again prove helpful in this connection. One respondent, for example, who had changed from "can't decide" to disagreement with the statement that "It would be a good idea if more business concerns would refuse to hire Jews" explained his change in the following way:

> I have been a little narrow-minded on that subject before. There was a time in my life when I sort of resented other nationalities. Maybe I still do; I don't know. That was in my younger days, though. *I've changed somewhat because I've heard lectures and listened to talk about it. I've read more about other people and I've been listening and getting other people's views. We have been hearing a lot more about this question recently and I've been thinking about it.*

Here is a respondent whose personal experiences have led him to develop a less prejudiced attitude toward Jews. He has attended lectures and engaged in conversations which have made him less "resentful of other nationalities" than he was in his younger days, or, as a matter of fact, than he was six months previously.

In this case, then, the personal experience led to a more favorable attitude. But another respondent had very different personal experiences which led her to develop a negative attitude on the very same question. She had originally disagreed with the statement about hiring Jews, but when this question was asked in the course of the intensive interview, she agreed with it. Her explanation for this change was as follows:

> (Can you think why you might have disagreed last time?) Well, I don't know. I didn't know about this Jewish clerk in my daughter's office then. *But after talking with my daughter about it, she saying that they're all lazy and all that, well...*

A conversation with her daughter, intervening between the two interviews, changed this respondent's original positive attitude to a more negative one.

These two cases help us understand how real changes in attitude can still result in a constant distribution of attitude. Our respondents are subject to very different kinds of pressures - in terms of their personal contacts and experiences - so that a change in one direction experienced by one individual is very likely to be balanced by a change in the opposite direction for another individual.

The highly personal nature of the events which seem effective in producing changes in attitude was also observed in connection with other questions in the Baltimore Study. It appeared, in that study, that it was the immediate experiences of the individual, rather than more remote events, which brought about many of the changes which we observed. For example, one woman who first agreed and then subsequently disagreed that "Generally speaking, Negroes are lazy and ignorant," made the following comment:

> (Do you ever remember agreeing with this question?) No, unless it was done at the time right after I came up here and this *colored man came up to the door and was very fresh. But I've had several colored girls come up and work for me and they've been very nice.*

Here we see the source of both the original negative attitude and of the present positive one. We note that the respondent was reacting in each case not to some general information about an important event, but rather to her own very limited contacts with, first, an unidentified Negro man, and later with Negro servants.

Finally, we quote from still another case to show that some of the change noted in connection with the items designed as personality measures can be accounted for through experiences of the individual respondent. The subject in question originally agreed, but later disagreed, that "Any leader should be strict with people under him in order to gain their respect." He explained this change as the result of a special training course which he attended:

> I disagree with that. We have programs of foremanship, which all emphasize the doubtfulness of that statement. I thought I disagreed with that question before, but I don't remember. I must have changed my mind. *I guess that foreman training must have had some effect.*

II. SYSTEMATIC EXPERIMENTATION

These qualitative materials from existing panel studies, inconclusive as they were, encouraged us to believe that systematic investigation would reveal the significant role played by mood in the stability of responses to repeated questions. Accordingly, we undertook the development of an experiment in which it might be possible to see the way in which changes in attitudes paralleled changes in mood. As in the conflict experiment, our subjects were college students who were asked to respond to a paper-and-pencil test on two separate occasions.[3] But, unlike the conflict questions which we knew our subjects could answer, we were not at all sure about their ability to report current mood states. A great part of our preliminary effort, therefore, was devoted to devising questions which would facilitate such reports.

The Measurement of Mood States

The questionnaire, which was exactly the same in both the original test and the retest, opened with a series of questions concerning the mood of the respondent at the time of each interview. In order to make sure that the subjects would answer in terms of their present mood, the schedule contained the following admonition:

> As you know from your own experience, everyone has 'ups and downs' in mood. We want to find out how you feel about yourself and life in general today. We don't want you to answer in terms of how you feel 'usually' or 'most of the time' but how you feel today.

We wanted the respondents to indicate their mood states with precision. Accordingly, we made use of barometer scales, rather than preestablished answer categories. The four mood questions on which we relied most heavily requested the respondents to indicate, on such a scale, how they felt in certain respects. The first of these was at the same time the most general one, asking for an overall evaluation of "good spirits:"[4]

> (1) First of all, we would like to know whether you are in pretty good spirits or pretty bad spirits today.
>
> Below is a kind of barometer of good feelings. 0 represents the worst spirits you've ever been in; 100 the best. Where would you put yourself today? (Draw a line through the place on the scale which represents how you feel.)
>
> 0 50 100
>
> Very bad spirits Very good spirits

The remaining three questions were designed to probe feelings along the specific dimensions of irritability-placidity, optimism-pessimism, and, finally, expansiveness-contraction.

> (2) Next we'd like to know how *irritable* you feel today. For example, would you be annoyed if something relatively unimportant went wrong?
>
> (3) And how about your feelings of *optimism* or *pessimism?* At the present time do you have the feeling that things in your life are going pretty well or pretty poorly?
>
> (4) Finally, we know that people vary from day to day in their feelings of *physical well-being.* On some days they are listless and tired; on other days they are full of pep and feel like conquering the world. How do you feel in this respect today?

For each of these questions there was a barometer on which the respondent could indicate exactly how he felt.

All of the evidence at our disposal suggests that our subjects were able to report their mood states with some accuracy. None complained about difficulties in indicating their positions on the barometers; and, as our later analysis will show, their reports appear to be entirely meaningful.

There are certain aspects of these measurements of mood states which deserve discussion, however.

(1) Constancy of marginals of mood barometers

One of the most striking features of the four mood barometers is a phenomenon with which we are already familar namely, the fact that the marginal distributions of responses obtained in the two interviews resembled each other closely. Despite the fact that the two questionnaires were administered approximately one month apart, on each occasion roughly the same proportions of subjects assumed the same scale positions on the four questions.

In order to show this constancy most clearly and most simply, we divided each of the scales into nine segments, and the position of each respondent within one of these segments was then determined. Table 23 shows how the sample distributed itself on the four questions and at the two interviews:

Table 23

The marginals of the mood barometers are constant.

Scale	Good spirits		Irritability		Optimism		Well-being	
Values	Int. I	Int. II	Int. I	Int. II	Int. I	Int. II	Int. I	Int. II
0-15	1%	3%	4%	4%	2%	4%	2%	3%
16-25	2	3	3	4	4	3	5	2
26-35	5	5	6	7	5	3	5	6
36-45	9	7	8	9	7	9	8	10
46-55	14	15	18	14	20	20	18	16
56-65	12	10	12	14	15	14	10	12
66-75	26	21	15	15	17	17	18	19
76-85	20	25	16	18	17	17	19	19
86-100	11	11	18	15	13	13	15	13
Total	512	512	512	512	512	512	512	512

If we compare the first and second interview distributions for each of the questions we find very great similarity. In the light of later findings on internal fluctuations, this marginal constancy is quite important.

A second point of interest in Table 23 concerns the average positions chosen by our subjects. From these several distributions, it is apparent that few wanted to claim really bad moods. Each distribution is negatively skewed, with the median point far toward the upper end of the scale. To put it somewhat differently, in each case, more than 50 per cent of the subjects placed themselves above the halfway mark in mood.[5] This was especially true for the first question, the most general one asking for a summary evaluation of mood.

Without further information we can only speculate as to why this is the case. One possible explanation is that the answers reflect traditional American beliefs that it is "wrong" to be pessimistic and irritable. A second possible explanation, and one which has interesting implications, is that in a college population such as that studied individuals are indeed as well adjusted, on the average, as their answers suggest. Our subjects were young, they were well enough off to attend college, and so on; there is little reason, therefore, why they should not feel in good spirits and in a good mood generally.

(2) Fluctuations in mood

We are by now well enough acquainted with the phenomenon of constant marginals to know that these rarely mean the absence of internal variations. Indeed, when we compare the first and second interview responses to any of these mood questions, we find rather wide fluctuations. Consider, for example, the way in which our subjects evaluated their "good spirits" in the two interviews:

Table 24

There is considerable fluctuation between the first and second interview in evaluations of good spirits.

Interview II									
86-100	-	-	2	2	8	5	14	11	15
76-85	-	2	4	13	13	14	38	28	15
66-75	-	3	5	15	13	12	33	21	6
56-65	-	1	4	4	8	9	13	10	5
46-55	-	2	6	5	17	7	16	16	7
36-45	-	-	2	1	3	9	9	10	3
26-35	-	-	-	4	4	4	9	4	2
16-25	-	1	-	-	2	1	6	2	1
0-15	3	1	1	1	2	1	3	1	-
	0-15	16-25	26-35	36-45	46-55	56-65	66-75	76-85	86-100
	Interview I								

While there is a positive correlation between first and second interview responses, there is great internal variation at the same time. Many respondents who said at first that they were in good spirits later felt in low spirits; many who said originally that they were in a bad mood had improved by the time of the second interview. The same pattern holds for the other barometer questions as well.[6]

(3) Measurement of mood change

It is these fluctuations in mood which interest us especially. If we are to be able to study the parallel changes in mood and attitude, then we must have some way of classifying respondents into those who have and those who have not experienced a shift in mood.

Many different measures of mood change come to mind. We might, of course, make use of the kind of material presented in Table 24 but this, quite obviously, would prove to be unwieldy. The measure which we finally adopted was suggested by latent structure analysis.[7] It turned out that answers to the four mood items seemed to be determined by a single underlying variable. When latent structure analysis was carried out, we found that the empirical data could be very well described by a dichotomous structure.[8] We were thus able to distinguish those whose answers to the four general mood questions indicated good mood both times (the + + group), those who shifted from a good to a bad mood (the + - group), those who shifted from a bad to a good mood (the - + group), and, finally, those whose responses suggested a consistently bad mood (the - - group). Table 25 shows that our respondents distributed themselves fairly evenly in these four groups, with the persons of constant mood only slightly more numerous than those changing in either direction:

Table 25

The sample is fairly evenly divided among the four mood classes.

		Interview I		
		Good mood	Bad mood	Total
Interview II	Good mood	171	103	274
	Bad mood	114	126	240
	Total	285	229	514

We note, incidentally, that even though the change classes are well populated, the marginal distribution of mood is constant from one interview to the next.

This is the measure of mood change on which we shall rely most heavily throughout the balance of our discussion.

Awareness of Mood Change

Our experiences with the four barometer questions satisfied us that our subjects could report their moods at any particular instant and that they would indicate different positions on the mood scales if any change had taken place between the two interviews. But we wanted to know, in addition, how aware they were of their shifts in mood, and of pressures bringing them about. While investigation of such awareness is not central to our basic hypothesis regarding the relationship between mood change and attitude change, it is of sufficient interest to detain us briefly.

(1) Pressures for mood change

In our earlier discussion of existing panel materials, we considered the way in which molecular pressures, as we called them, led to attitude changes. It appears that the same kinds of influences - highly personal experiences and contacts - also bring about fluctuations in mood. But perhaps of even greater importance than the effectiveness of such molecular pressures is the fact that most individuals are aware of their operation.

All of the subjects were asked whether "anything particular happened in the last few days which put you in a particularly good or bad mood." Answers to this question are reported in Table 26:

Table 26

The proportion of persons reporting pressure toward good mood dropped between the first and second interviews.

	Interview I	Interview II
No, nothing special has happened	36%	55%
Yes, something has happened which put me in *good* mood	37	22
Yes, something has happened which put me in *bad* mood	27	23
Total cases	485	485

This was one of the few questions in which the results of the two interviews were substantially different. We note, further, that the change comes about through a drop in the number of individuals experiencing pressures toward more favorable moods, and an increase in the number saying that "nothing special" had happened. The possible reasons for this shift deserve some discussion.

By considering the nature of the pressures which our subjects believed influential in changing their moods and the context of the second interview, we can develop a plausible explanation as to why there were fewer persons reporting pressures toward positive change. First of all. we know from the way in which our respondents described what had happened to them that only "special events" were considered influential. By and large, they referred to incidents which were unexpected or not routine. We can quote a variety of these to suggest their general character. For example, one girl who reported that she was in an especially good mood, explained:

> A special gentleman is coming for the weekend after saying he couldn't come.

Two other young girl students reported incidents in their love life which made them particularly unhappy. One said:

> The boy I love broke a promise, and I said we would have to stop seeing each other.

The other told us:

> My fiance called long distance to say that he was going into the Army.

Another of our subjects explained that he was in a bad mood because "A Rorschach (test), self-scored, indicates an immature personality." Still other respondents reported accidents which had put them in especially bad moods:

> The refrigerator broke down, ruining a lot of food; and the service company's efficiency in attending to it is poor.

However general these incidents may be in the population as a whole, all of them were unexpected and of a special nature for the particular individuals who reported them.

Secondly, the retest questionnaire was administered, in most cases, as the time for final examinations approached; as a matter of fact, one group of subjects was asked to fill out the retest form during the last meeting of the course. Now the imminence of examination period is not likely to be classified as a "special event;" it is expected, and, in a sense, routine. It was not often pointed out as something conducive to bad moods, therefore.[9] But it may be that the general oppression connected with approaching examinations makes "special events" which would otherwise put the subject in a good mood seem relatively unimportant and minor. That is, an unexpected visit from a boy in whom one is interested may not produce the same kind of exhilaration as it might if it came at a time when one was not vaguely worried about examinations.

The result which interests us especially, however, is that individuals are apparently aware of influences making for changes in mood. In the (+ -) group, where mood deteriorated between the first and second interviews, most of the respondents who reported that something had happened indicated that it was an event which led them to develop a bad mood; exactly the reverse is true in the (- +) group:

Table 27

Respondents who deteriorate in mood report events leading to a bad mood; respondents who improve in mood report events leading to a good mood.

Report of Special Event Preceding Second Interview	Mood Class (+ -)	Mood Class (- +)
"Something happened which put me in a *bad* mood"	45	3
"Something happened which put me in a *good* mood"	12	35
Total cases	57	38

While there are few cases, the trend is clear. The mood changers spoke of molecular pressures conducive to their present mood states.

(2) Self-estimates of mood constancy

While these college students seem aware of recent events and incidents bringing about changes in mood, they appear less sensitive to general characteristics of their mood fluctuations. This is especially true of their estimates of their own mood constancy.

Each respondent was asked "Compared to most people you know, would you consider yourself a person of changing moods, or one whose moods remain fairly constant?" We know, from their responses to the several mood questions, whether or not they changed. It is therefore possible to compare these self-estimates with the way in which the respondents actually behaved.

Our common-sense expectation is that subjects who consider themselves more changeable in mood than the average person will turn out to be so when their behavior is studied. It is therefore somewhat paradoxical that this is not the case. As a matter of fact, we find that those who say they are especially changeable are slightly more *constant* than respondents who tell us of their general mood constancy:

Table 28

Those who consider themselves changeable show greater constancy in their actual behavior.

According to Actual Behavior	According to Self-Estimate	
	Changeable	Constant
Changeable	40%	44%
Constant	60	56
Total cases	176	258

The expected correspondence between self-evaluation and actual behavior is not found.

It is not easy to interpret this finding. But one fact, perhaps of relevance in this connection, is that those saying they are more changeable than the average person have definitely worse moods than those saying they believe themselves to be relatively constant:

Table 29

Those who consider themselves changeable are in less good mood than those who consider themselves constant.

Among Those Who Consider Selves	Percent Classified as Having A Good Mood at Time of	
	Interview I	Interview II
Constant	63	60
Changeable	44	41

It is possible that persons who are in an especially bad mood cannot visualize that as more than a temporary state, and therefore characterize themselves as more changeable than the average person. Because they *want* their mood to change, they think of themselves as being particularly unstable in this respect. These are speculations which deserve further investigation. But the finding indicates, in any event, that self-evaluations of constancy cannot be substituted for observed behavior.

So far we have considered various aspects of mood and mood changes; we have not investigated how these are related to other attitudes, however. It is to this problem which we now turn.

Mood Shifts and Attitude Change

It makes good sense to suppose that the way in which an individual feels at a particular moment will be reflected in his attitudes. If something has irritated him, we expect him to be more aggressive than he would be under different conditions; if some event has put him in especially good spirits, we expect him to be more jovial than he would be otherwise. From this we can expect that attitude *changes* will parallel *changes* in mood. If an individual is definitely more irritated today than he was yesterday, we anticipate that he will show evidence of increased aggressiveness. [10]

Perhaps it is the very plausibility of these expectations which explains why they have not been systematically investigated. It may be that we all take the matter so much for granted that we do not consider research necessary. In any event, we have been able to find only scattered references to the role of mood in attitude formation and change.

(1) Existing speculations

Occasionally we find mood referred to as a factor making difficult any literal interpretation of data. Thus, Carl Hovland and his associates point out that mood changes can distort experimental results, particularly when the experimental design is such that each individual serves as his own control. As they put it:[11]

> "A further possible difficulty with using each man as his own control is that *obtained shifts in response due to transient mood changes may be correlated with evaluations of the film, giving rise to a spurious factor in the analysis.* Suppose, for example, a respondent filling out the "after" questionnaire in the study of the "Battle of Britain" feels in a generous mood. As a result he gives more pro-British answers than before, and at the same time gives a favorable evaluation of the film. Another respondent with an opposite mood may swell the ranks of those who changed to more anti-British responses and at the same time give the film an unfavorable evaluation. The spurious factor is this correlation of errors in responses to the two kinds of questions, those measuring effects and those measuring evaluations. It seems probable that this spurious factor is small or absent - i.e., that absence of correlation in errors of measurement would be the general rule. To the extent that such a factor is present, however, it cannot be separated from correlation of true evaluations and true changes in opinion if one merely uses each man as

> his own control. This is one of the weaknesses inherent in correlational as contrasted with experimental analysis."

It will be noted that these authors consider the role of mood changes, which lead to "errors in response," minor.

While these authors speculated that mood might play a role in their results, they had no concrete evidence of its actual operation. In a second study there was some incidental data concerning the role of mood. In her study of factors related to changes in attitude toward Negroes and Jews, Jeanne Watson found much the same result that we did in some of the intensive interviews collected for the Baltimore Study:[12]

> "Several people reported that a decided increase or decrease in happiness had occurred about the time of the change (in attitude). As might have been expected, greater happiness was associated with positive change toward Negroes, Jews, or both; it was associated with either a general personality reorganization or a generally liberalized outlook on the world; and it resulted in an attitude which was both integrated and salient."

As she discusses them, Watson seems to have in mind mood changes of a more permanent nature than those which concern us. Nonetheless, her observations led her to formulate a hypothesis for further research very similar to that being investigated in the present study:

> "*Hypothesis:* An increase in the general level of happiness and satisfaction may be followed by an actively favorable attitude toward minority groups."

A number of psychologists have studied the behavioral and subjective correlates of mood. One of the earliest of these studies found that there was a relationship between estimated mood and recall of pleasant and unpleasant experiences.[13] In another study, subjects were asked to write down the names of persons. Those diagnosed as optimistic tended to list a large proportion of persons whom they liked and a small proportion of persons whom they disliked; subjects classified as pessimistic showed the opposite trend.[14] Johnson found that a euphoric state tended to be correlated with greater frequency of spontaneous comments, greater social confidence, a feeling of increased physical energy, and so on.[15]

One of the most recent of these studies is that carried out by Bousfield.[16] He set out to investigate two interrelated hypotheses:

> "(a) With pleasant mood there is a facilitation of verbal associative responses having pleasant affective value. (b) With unpleasant mood there is a facilitation of verbal associative responses having unpleasant affective value."[17]

One group of subjects was asked to think of pleasant events and situations; a second group was asked to think of unpleasant events and situations; and a third group was assigned a neutral task. Before starting on the experimental task, subjects were asked to provide self-ratings of their feeling states, using a barometer somewhat similar to that employed in the present study. The results tended to confirm Bousfield's first hypothesis: among those assigned the task of reporting pleasant events, the subjects who had signified their good mood listed more events than those indicating a bad mood. The reverse trend was present only to a slight degree among those asked to recall unpleasant events.

While all of these studies dealt with the correlates of mood at one particular time, none of them considered mood *changes* and the way these might be related to *changes* in the correlated behavior. So far as we have been able to determine, there is only one study which made these questions the object of direct study. In what can be considered, without overstatement, a trail-blazing study, Rex. B. Hersey studied emotional cycles in a group of workers, and related these mood cycles to changes in productivity.[18] The subjects were studied for approximately one year, each being interviewed an *average of four times a day.* Hersey did not make use of any barometric scale; instead he had his subjects describe their moods with appropriate adjectives, to which he then assigned arbitrary values ranging from +6 to -6. Although few subjects participated in the study, the cyclical movement of each individual's mood is very noticeable.[19] Hersey found, further, that changes in mood were related to changes in productivity: workers tended to produce more when in positive emotional states than they did when in negative states.[20]

It is difficult to understand why, in the twenty years since Hersey first published his findings, there has apparently been no effort to carry them further.

(2) Experimental investigation of mood

In order to study the role of mood systematically, it was again necesssry to formulate more precisely just what we expected. Our basic hypothesis can be stated as follows:

> Different responses to a particular attitude question can be expected if the several interviews are obtained when the individual is in different phases of his mood cycle.

Diagramatically, our hypothesis can be expressed in this way:

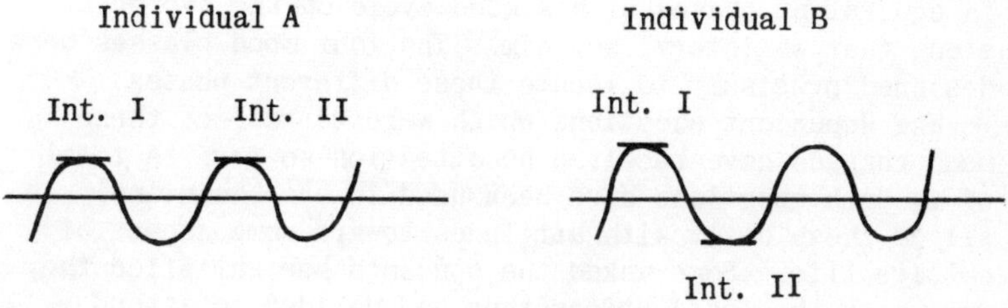

Individual A

Int. I Int. II

Individual B

Int. I

Int. II

Individual A was interviewed at two points in time when he happened to be in exactly equivalent phases of his mood cycle. Individual B, on the other hand, was questioned at times when he was in quite different phases.

Individual A thus had similar "response sets" at the time of both interviews. Individual B did not; accordingly we expect him to give different answers to a question repeated on both occasions.

This hypothesis rests on a number of assumptions. The first of these is that individuals experience mood cycles of the kind observed by Hersey. The second assumption is that, at any given moment, different individuals are in different phases of their respective mood cycles. Finally, we assume that the emotional state in which an individual finds himself will influence his behavior and will reflect itself in his opinions and sentiments.

Because we made only two observations rather than the large number required to establish the existence of mood cycles, the first assumption cannot be tested by our data. We have presented some evidence bearing on the second one, namely, the fact that our respondents indicated moods which differed (a) from the moods of other persons interviewed at the same time, and (b) from their own moods at a different time. Some evidence for the third assumption will be discussed in the following pages.

We have already devoted considerable attention to procedures for determining whether or not an individual was in equivalent phases of his mood cycle on the two occasions that we interviewed him. The four mood classes were designed precisely to locate these different phases.

The dependent questions which were to reflect these mood changes have received no attention so far. A total of 14 such questions have been used in our basic analysis. All of these dealt with attitudes toward some aspect of college life. Some asked the students how satisfied they were with the institutions they had decided to attend. For example:

> How well do you think your school is preparing you for the work you intend to do after college?
>
> -- Very well
>
> -- Fairly well
>
> -- Not so well
>
> -- Not at all well

We also asked about attitudes toward professors, satisfaction with classroom discussion, and so on.

In other questions we tried to find out how aggressive our subjects were toward their fellow students:

> Would you say that there are some kinds of students who make themselves obnoxious?
>
> -- No, none that I can think of
>
> -- Yes

In still other questions we made an effort to learn about the students' own feelings of adequacy in the school situation:

> At the present moment, what are your feelings about the progress you are making in your studies?
>
> -- At the present time, I'm completely satisfied with the progress I'm making.
>
> -- At the present time I'm doing satisfactory work, but I would like to do better.
>
> -- I'm passing, but that's about all.
>
> -- I'm not sure I'm passing my courses.

Along similar lines, we asked them how much they worried about their studies, and whether they felt at ease in the classroom.[21]

Our hypothesis can be confirmed only if answers to these questions reflect to some degree the respondents' mood states. That is, we shall find that an attitude change experienced by an individual will parallel his mood shift between two periods of time only if the answers given by a group at one time are correlated with their mood states at that moment.[22] In our data this condition was met only to a disappointingly small degree. Although the mood items themselves were highly inter correlated, they were not equally related to the attitude questions.[23]

This makes our end result - the parallel shift of mood and attitude - less clearcut than it might otherwise have been. In Table 30 we report the average proportion of respondents in each mood class answering the 14 questions favorably in the first interview and then again in the second.[24] We would consider our hypothesis fairly well established if we observed the following. We expect that the (+ +) group will give a large proportion of responses expressing optimism and other positive feelings, and that this proportion will remain fairly constant from one interview to the next. We expect that the (- -) group will give considerably fewer positive responses, but that their less favorable attitudes will remain constant from one interview to the next. We expect very different patterns from those who have experienced mood shifts. In the (+ -) group, we look for *first* interview responses similar to those in the (+ +) group, and *second* interview responses similar to those of the (--) subjects.[25] In the (- +) group we expect exactly the opposite: their *first* interview responses should be similar to those of the (- -) group; their *second* interview responses should be similar to those given by the (+ +) group. Table 30 shows that, on the average, this tendency exists:

Table 30

There is some tendency for attitude changes to parallel mood shifts.

Average Percent of Favorable Responses to 14 Attitude Questions[26]

	In Good Mood at First Interview		In Bad Mood at First Interview	
	Int. I	Int. II	Int. I	Int. II
In Good Mood at Second Interview	<u>72.4</u>	<u>74.0</u>	69.0	<u>78.8</u>
In Bad Mood at Second Interview	<u>78.7</u>	69.8	67.6	67.7

We note that, on the average, those in a good mood at the time of either interview gave more favorable answers to the 14 dependent questions than did those who were in a bad mood. (The relevant figures have been underscored.) This indicates that the moods of the respondents were reflected, to some extent, in their answers to these questions. The degree of correlation is not large, however.

The more important point is that mood shifts seem to be reflected in attitude changes. Those with constant moods showed, again on the average, a constant level of favorable attitude; those with shifting moods varied in attitude level.

The results of Table 30 are not very clear-cut. The differences are not large, and, when we examine responses to each of the 14 questions individually, we discover that they are not always consistent.[27] There was one series of questions, however, where the parallel between mood and attitude changes was very clear. We asked the subjects how they would react in three annoying situations - being made to wait for a lunch date,[28] seeing someone push ahead in a line waiting to get into a movie theater, being jostled by a stranger in a subway. These questions differed from those we have considered not only in their content, but also in their form. They were not asked as attitude questions, inquiring into what the respondent believed should be done in each situation. Instead, they asked how he would react if he felt as he did at that moment. For example, one question read as follows:[29]

> Suppose that you and a friend were standing in line waiting to get into a movie and noticed that a couple had sneaked in ahead of you.
>
> If I felt the way I feel today, I would
>
> -- Just ignore the couple, and continue to wait in line.
>
> -- Speak politely to the couple about their unsocial behavior and suggest that they go to the end of the line where they belong.

-- I would tell my friend loud enough for them to hear just what I thought of people like that.

-- I would make an issue of it and try to make the people move to the end of the line where they belong.

In this form mood was emphasized more than it had been in the questions dealing with college life.[30] When we examine the average number of aggressive reactions given by the different mood classes in each interview, we find a marked tendency for attitude shifts (or, more properly, changes in reactions) to follow mood changes.

Table 31

There is a marked tendency for changes in reactions to follow mood shifts.

	Average Percent of Unaggressive Reactions to 3 Annoying Situations[31]			
	In Good Mood at First Interview		In Bad Mood at First Interview	
	Int. I	Int. II	Int. I	Int. II
In Good Mood at Second Interview	<u>73.7</u>	<u>70.0</u>	53.3	<u>70.0</u>
In Bad Mood at Second Interview	<u>66.3</u>	48.0	53.7	52.3

Again we have underscored the figures obtained from those in a good mood at the time of either interview. We see here that the relationship between mood and aggressiveness of reaction is quite marked: considerably more aggressive reactions are found among those in bad mood.

Further, we find that changes in reaction are quite closely related to changes in mood. Those in a consistently good mood show a constant lack of aggression; those in a consistently bad mood are constant in their unfavorable responses. The two groups of mood changers reveal degrees of aggressiveness which correspond to their moods at the time of each interview.

When the dependent question is one in which present feelings are themselves stressed, the results are considerably more clear-cut.

(3) Attitude change and degree of fluctuation in mood

Up to this point we have not considered the fact that our subjects experienced varying *degrees* of shift in mood. If we recall the results of Table 24 we note that there were extreme and moderate shifts. Some of the subjects changed from what may have seemed to them the depths of despair to a fairly high level of optimism; others experienced just the opposite kind of shift, from a very good to a very bad mood; in other cases, the shift was not so pronounced; and in still other instances, there was no change at all.

Now it seems reasonable to expect that the probability of attitude change will be related to the degree of change in mood. If we are correct in assuming that attitude change parallels mood change, then those who experienced a very marked shift in mood are more likely to change in their attitudes than are those who experienced only a minor shift from, let us say, moderate optimism to great optimism.

In order to explore this possibility it was first necessary to devise a different measure of mood change. In the previous analysis we considered only whether or not the subjects had placed themselves on both occasions within the same half of the dichotomized mood scale. Now, however, we must set aside this gross measure of change, and develop another which distinguishes different amounts, as well as directions, of change. The new measure which we propose for the present analysis was arrived at in the following way. As we indicated earlier, each of the mood barometers was divided into nine segments, representing different positions along a scale of 0-100. The amount of change attributed to the individual depended on the number of positions which he moved upward or downward between the two interviews. In this way we were able to distinguish five degrees of mood change.[32]

(1) *Marked deterioration of mood:* a downward shift of 3 or more positions on the mood scale

(2) *Moderate deterioration of mood:* a downward shift of 1 or 2 positions on the mood scale

(3) *No change:* no change in position on the mood scale

(4) *Moderate improvement in mood:* an upward shift of 1 or 2 positions on the mood scale

(5) *Marked improvement in mood:* an upward shift of 3 or more positions on the mood scale.

Each individual was classified with regard to his change on each of the four mood barometers separately.[33] The different degrees of mood change were then related to shifts in expressed attitudes. We started with the 14 questions about college life used in our previous analysis. (See Table 30 above.) As Table 32 indicates, there is a parallel between degree of mood change and the likelihood of attitude change. The greater the amount of change in mood, the greater the probability of an attitude shift.

Table 32

Changes in attitudes toward college life parallel to some extent the direction and degree of mood change

Degree and direction of mood change	Average change in percentage of favorable responses to 14 attitude questions: "Good spirits"	"Irritability"	"Optimism"	"Physical well-being"
Marked deterioration	-1.7	-3.6	-2.8	-2.9
Moderate deterioration	-1.9	-1.6	-1.1	-1.4
No change	- .8	+1.9	+ .5	+ .8
Moderate improvement	+ .4	+2.2	+1.6	+ .5
Marked improvement	+2.4	+ .2	+1.9	+2.3

In order to interpret Table 32 correctly, some further explanation is required. Actually this table shows four separate relationships, that between change on each of the mood barometers and average change in favorable answers to the 14 attitude questions. A negative figure indicates that the proportion of persons in that particular category of mood change responding favorably to the attitude questions *declined*, on the average, between the first and second interviews. A positive figure, on the other hand, indicates that the proportion of subjects responding favorably *increased* between the two interviews. And the larger the figure, whether positive or negative, the higher the proportion of persons expressing different attitudes on the two occasions.

Examination of Table 32 indicates, then, that the probability of attitude change parallels, in general, the degree of shift in mood. Although the differences are not always large, nor entirely consistent, subjects who had experienced marked deterioration in mood on any one of the mood barometers generally showed the greatest likelihood of negative attitude change, while those who had experienced marked improvement in mood were most likely to exhibit positive change in attitude.

In our previous analysis we found that these reactions to college life were less sensitive to mood changes than were responses to annoying situations in which the students might find themselves. The same is true in our present analysis. Degrees of mood change are more clearly reflected in varying reactions to the situations of being "stood up" on a date, of having someone push ahead in a line waiting to enter a theater, and of being jostled in a subway. This is shown in Table 33.

Table 33

Aggressive reactions to annoying situations are directly related to the direction and degree of mood change

Degree and direction of mood change	Average change in percentage of *un*aggressive reactions to 3 annoying situations			
	"Good spirits"	"Irritability	"Optimism"	"Physical well-being"
Marked deterioration	-13.0	-14.3	-10.3	- 9.7
Moderate deterioration	-13.7	- 9.7	- 6.3	-10.0
No change	+ 1.3	+ 1.7	- 1.7	- 6.7
Moderate improvement	+ 3.0	+ .7	- 2.3	+ 7.3
Marked improvement	+16.3	+16.3	+14.3	+ 9.7

In these three questions, the relationships between mood changes and attitude change are quite striking. Generally, those who experienced a marked deterioration in mood are considerably more likely than any other students to exhibit an increase in aggressive reactions, while, conversely, those who experienced a marked improvement in mood are very much more likely to show a decrease in aggressive reactions.

Program for Further Research

Partly because our original hypothesis seemed so obvious and plausible it deserves further study. We should like to find out why it was that our results did not always turn out to have greater clarity or consistency. Most progress is likely to come through the introduction of certain refinements which we had in mind only vaguely at the time that the original investigation was planned.

(1) Relative objectivity of the questions

The first refinement pertains to the dependent questions on which change is to be observed. We know that there are certain kinds of questions - those dealing with facts or information, and perhaps also those eliciting stereotypic responses - which are not likely to be answered in terms of present emotional states.[34] At the other extreme are attitude questions which are answered almost wholly in terms of present feelings of optimism-pessimism, irritability-placidity, and so on.

An important extension of our procedure would be to see whether changes on these "objective" questions are less highly correlated with mood shifts than are changes on the "subjective" questions. We kept this possibility in mind when planning our research. For example, we asked our respondents two questions about their college grades. The first of these asked about the average grade they had *received* for their work during the preceding semester; the second asked about the average they *expected* for the then current semester. It was our belief that mood would play only a minor role in answers to the first question, but a major role in answers to the second. The results were not so clear-cut, however. While there was greater instability in answers to the question on expected grades, the patterns of change showed no consistent relationship to mood shifts.

At the time that we were making up the schedule, we also made an effort to predict which of the dependent questions would be most likely and which least likely to reflect mood. Examination of the correlation between mood at any one time and answers to these various questions indicates, however, that our predictions were not entirely successful.

Any program of future research should start by devising questions which reflect moods in varying degrees. One crucial test of our basic hypothesis would be if it did *not* hold true for relatively "objective" questions.

(2) Tendency to generalize mood

The second refinement pertains to characteristics of the subjects being studied. There are undoubtedly some individuals who compartmentalize their feelings, so that emotional feelings in one area do not affect emotional states in other areas. In other individuals there is undoubtedly a tendency to *generalize* moods. What they feel at a particular moment about their work situation will color how they feel about their personal lives.

The presence or absence of this tendency permits a second extension of our basic procedure. It is clear that, if our hypothesis is correct, the correlation of mood and attitude changes should be higher among those who tend to generalize their moods than among those who do not. In the latter group answers to questions about college life are not so likely to reflect unhappy love or financial worries or fatigue.

We kept this possibility in mind also when devising the interview schedule to be used in our investigation. But again our success was limited. It proved very difficult to find a question, or even a series of questions, which would indicate the presence or absence of this characteristic. This seems to require more intensive procedures; it is not an appropriate topic for study in a self-administered paper-and-pencil test.

We did make one attempt in this direction, however. We asked each of our subjects the following question:

> When annoying things happen to you (like being made to wait, or being jostled in a subway, or watching people sneak ahead of you in line), does it have an influence on how you feel the rest of the day?
>
> -- I usually am not annoyed by the kind of minor things that annoy others.
>
> -- I forget minor annoyances as soon as they happen
>
> -- Minor annoyances have an effect on me for an hour or so, but not much longer than that
>
> -- A minor annoyance in the morning usually spoils most of my day

Through the answers to this question we hoped to find out which subjects experienced a *time* generalization of mood. That is, instead of determining whether moods were generalized from one *area* to another (which proved to be impossible in a self-administered questionnaire), we tried to learn the extent to which moods persisted in time. Our expectation was that respondents saying that their moods lasted would show a higher correlation between mood and attitude change than would be found among other subjects. Here again the results were confusing; they will not be reported therefore.

Any future investigation of mood influences should bear in mind the possible relevance of this characteristic, however. Whether or not it will be possible to devise appropriate questions to determine the presence or absence of this trait is itself a question for considerable further exploration.

CHAPTER 3

ROLE OF OTHER FACTORS

It is obvious, of course, that we cannot explain all turnover of response by reference to the two factors discussed so far. The processes which lead individuals to respond differently on different occasions to repeated questions are undoubtedly very complicated ones, which cannot be understood in terms of one or two factors only. And, while we concentrated on the role of psychological conflict and of changing moods, we were able, at the same time, to gain some preliminary insights into the influence of other factors. One of these is interest in and concern with the topic under investigation; the second is the nature of the questions to which responses are obtained.

I. THE ROLE OF INTEREST AND CONCERN

Survey analysts are becoming increasingly aware that the respondent's interest in or concern with a topic is a significant dimension of his attitude on the issue, and that it is a dimension which must be taken into account when responses to survey questions are analyzed. One reason for this is that those who lack interest in the topic are likely to give perfunctory responses, and, in the terms of our analysis, such perfunctory responses are unstable. They are likely to vary from one occasion to another.

In order to understand better how interest and stability of response are related, we must clarify the meaning and implications of the absence of interest.

Lack of Interest and Perfunctory Responses

It sometimes happens that issues which seem of vital importance to the research organizations sponsoring particular investigations are matters of complete indifference to many of the respondents included in the study. It will be recalled that the second interview in the Baltimore Study took place immediately after Israel had declared itself an independent state and fighting between Arabs and Jews had broken out. Despite the objective importance of these events, we found a number of subjects discounting their significance entirely. One respondent, asked at the outset of the intensive interview whether he remembered having been questioned previously, commented:

> Yes, I remember taking the poll before. It didn't seem to add up to me. I didn't see exactly what they were driving at. There were a lot of questions certainly. *I didn't see that they were burning questions at the time. There were a lot of questions about Jews and then some that had to do with Palestine. Perhaps the poll taker had an old poll or was several months behind.* I don't know. Since then the Palestine question has been settled. That is not too important today.

For this respondent the issue of Palestine was so unimportant that he could only conclude that an interview dealing with it was in some way a mistake. The only explanation as to why someone would ask him questions on this issue was that they were using an "old poll" or were trying to catch up on back work.

Another of the intensive interviews ended up on a similar note:

> You seldom hear the Palestine problem discussed, and *I don't think about it at all.* I know that I should; it is to my own interest to know what is going on in the world. Then I could give you a fair opinion on it. *I am more interested in domestic affairs.* I miss a man in the house to discuss things with. You can really get so much with discussion when you talk with them. We never discuss it here. *I don't see where the Palestine situation would really affect us.*

This respondent has a feeling that she should express some interest in the Palestine situation; but, since there is no "man in the house" to stimulate that interest, she does not see the relevance of events in Palestine.

Lack of interest in an issue can be described as a failure to give the matter any attention.[1] This comes out quite clearly in the preceding comment: "I don't think about it at all", "we never discuss it here", and so on. This fact has a variety of implications. The person without interest is likely to give *perfunctory* responses. If he has not given previous thought to the topic about which he is questioned, it is very unlikely that he has any real basis for answering one way rather than another. That he answers at all can be considered a response to the interview situation rather than to the specific question; he obliges the interviewer by selecting an answer category. The following comment shows this very clearly:

> (Do you remember ever feeling any differently about this?) *It never bothered me. I just answered the questions and never gave it a second thought. Maybe I wouldn't have answered if I had thought about it.* I told her (the interviewer) at the time it wasn't going to amount to a row of pins. (How important is this question to you?) It is nothing to me. I am too old to take stock in that. Nothing bothers me.

It is quite obvious here that the respondent answered because she was required to. In fact, she warned the interviewer that her opinions would not amount "to a row of pins." On more sober reflection she believes that, had she thought about the questions when they were asked originally, she would not have answered them at all.

It is not difficult to see that perfunctory responses are unstable. Since it is almost a matter of chance whether the respondent will answer "yes" or "no" there is great likelihood that he will respond one way on one occasion and a completely different way on a second occasion.

The unstable character of perfunctory responses was brought out quite explicitly in some of the intensive interviews.

> (According to the interviewer who spoke to you before, she said that at that time you disagreed with this question. What do you think about that?) I don't know. The day she was here I was busy. The interviewer took so long. *I probably answered in*

> *any old way...*(The Jews have set up a new Jewish state in part of Palestine. Do you approve or disapprove of this action by the Jews?) Well, I really don't know anything about it. (Well, what's your general feeling?) Oh, I don't know. (According to the interviewer who spoke to you last time, you disapproved then. What do you think about that?) I don't remember much about it. *I was in such a hurry, and I was hoping she would go.* I remembered a lady here before, and I wondered why the heck they were asking over and over again the same things.

Here we see quite dramatically how lack of interest functions to produce turnover in response. The subject who is busy, who is in "such a hurry", answers in "any old way". so that the interview will end. And answers given in this fashion are likely to be different from one interview to another.

Another respondent, asked to explain a change in answer to one question dealing with Negroes, replied:

> *Well, I don't think about that question enough to have any real definite opinion.*

Perhaps the most succinct statement of the relationship between lack of interest and instability of response is contained in the following comment:

> (Do you feel you might answer these questions a different way another time?) Well, on the Palestine questions *I might answer one way one time and another way the next, because I'm not interested and don't know enough about it.* The only thing I read in the papers is the comics and sport pages.

These qualitative materials give some indication of the importance of interest and concern in making for stable responses. In survey materials the phenomenon itself stands out just as clearly, even though it is more difficult to see the process through which the factors are related.

Self-Evaluations of Interest and Stability of Response

In survey work there are a number of different ways in which the interest of respondents can be gauged. Perhaps the most obvious method is to ask them directly how concerned they are with the problem area being discussed. This type of question is used with increasing frequency in modern polling work; while it is undoubtedly true that some respondents are unable or unwilling to place themselves in the correct interest categories, it has been found that, by and large, techniques of self-classification work adequately.[2]

The Cincinnati Study used several questions of this kind: panel members were asked to indicate how interested they were in the United Nations, in questions of our trade with foreign countries, in matters concerning the atom bomb. In general, those who said they had a high degree of interest in any of these topics were more stable in their answers to related attitude questions. Consider, for example, questions dealing with the control of the atom bomb. In addition to giving estimates of their interest in such questions, the respondents were asked whether they were in favor of some system of international control of the bomb.[3]

The relationship between interest in the problem and stability of answers is shown in Table 34:

Table 34

Those who express keen interest in the atom bomb answer a question on how it should be controlled with greater stability than is found on lower interest levels.

(Cincinnati Study)

	Index Value	Number of Cases
High education		
Keen interest	.10	104
Mild or no interest	.21	46
Low education		
Keen interest	.18	118
Mild or no interest	.22	60

The index used here is the familiar turnover index, used throughout Chapter 1. As usual, the higher the value of the index the greater the amount of instability.

Within each of the educational groups, high interest is associated with high stability. We might comment briefly on why it is necessary to control educational level here. One of the most consistent findings in the analysis of turnover figures is that the better educated the respondent, the more likely it is that he will give consistent answers in successive interview waves. It is not entirely clear how this relationship should be interpreted. It may be that education is indicative of higher levels of interest; it may be that better educated respondents are able to sense the "correct" answers to most questions and consistently select these responses; it may be simply that they are better able to remember in a second interview how they answered the first time. Whatever the interpretation, the relationship itself is found so regularly that it must be taken into account. And since there is usually a relationship between education and interest it seems advisable to control education when studying whether greater interest is associated with greater stability.

It turns out, furthermore, that these self-estimates of interest are related to the stability of information levels as well. Panel members in the Cincinnati Study were asked a third question about the atom bomb, this one dealing with a point of information: "As far as you know, is it the job of the UN to deal with disarmament and the A-bomb?" As we might expect, those who expressed keen interest in news of the atom bomb were generally better informed about the role of the United Nations in controlling it. But what is more interesting in the present context is that those who claimed keen interest were also more stable in their levels of information(Table 35).

Manifestations of Interest and Stability of Response

Much the same sort of result is found when, instead of classifying our respondents according to the amount of interest which they claim to have, we categorize them on the basis of manifested interest. In general interest is not a passive attitude; it expresses itself in a variety of different behaviors. When we take these overt indications as the measure of interest we find again that those

Table 35

Those who are highly interested in the atom bomb are more consistently informed about the role of the UN in atomic energy control.

(Cincinnati Study)

	Index Value	Number of Cases
High education		
Keen interest	.12	97
Mild or no interest	.27	34
Low education		
Keen interest	.24	79
Mild or no interest	.50	20

who are more concerned with the issue around which the interviewing centers give more stable responses.

In the Elmira Study, for example, the panel members were asked whether, compared with other people they knew, they were more or less likely to be asked their opinion about political affairs. Those who said that they were more likely to be asked advice are also likely to be especially interested in political matters. When their answers to other political questions are contrasted with those given by respondents who say that they are as likely or less likely to be asked about political issues, we find that the "opinion leaders," as they are called, are more stable. (This is shown in Table 36.)

The question on which we observe turnover here asked the respondent whether he believed that the Democrats or Republicans would win the November election. Responses to this question followed the pattern which we described earlier. In both interviews, a majority of the subjects expected the Republicans to win, but between interviews there was shifting back and forth among individuals. We see in Table 36 that a part of this shifting can be accounted for by lack of interest or concern. While the differences are not large, especially among the less well educated, opinion leaders, those who manifest interest in political

Table 36

Those who manifest high interest through their function as opinion leaders are more stable in their attitudes to related questions than are the respondents who do not manifest interest.

(Elmira Study)

	Index Value	Number of Cases
High education		
Opinion leaders	.06	100
Others	.16	200
Low education		
Opinion leaders	.13	88
Others	.15	187

matters, show less variability. Their opinions are more definitely formed and therefore more stable.

Thus far we have taken as our indices of interest the self-estimates provided in answer to direct questions and the existence of certain behavior patterns which might be considered symptomatic of concern or interest. Still other indices are available to the survey analyst. Spontaneous mention of a topic in answer to a free answer question is often taken as evidence of concern or interest. And, when the appropriate data are available, we generally find that those who spontaneously mention an issue have more stable responses to related attitude questions. Thus in the Elmira Study, respondents were asked to indicate, without the aid of a checklist, what they considered the main issues in the presidential campaign.[4] A number of subjects spontaneously mentioned our foreign policy. The same respondents were also asked about their expectations concerning the probability of war,[5] a question which was repeated again in a later interview. This latter question was one of the few in which a marginal change was found; the proportion of respondents saying that they expected war increased somewhat between June and

October. Nonetheless, superimposed on or intermingled with this response to external events was the phenomenon which we have observed before - the apparently random shifting back and forth between one position and another. As Table 37 shows, interest helps once more to explain this:[6]

Table 37

Those who manifest interest in foreign affairs through the spontaneous mention of foreign policy as an important campaign issue are more stable in their expectations of war than are other respondents.

(Elmira Study)

	Index Value	Number of Cases
Spontaneous mention of foreign policy	.10	198
No spontaneous mention	.12	398

Other respondents, in stating what they considered important campaign issues, spontaneously referred to various labor problems. Elsewhere in the interview all of the panel members were asked their attitude toward labor unions,[7] another question which was repeated at a later date. Although the differences are not large, Table 38 shows once more that interest, as manifested by spontaneous references to the topic, is related to stable responses on the corollary question.

Were it possible to find other manifestations of interest in particular issues, we should expect similar relationships between degree of interest and stability of attitude toward the issue.

Inferred Interest and Stability of Response

The indices of interest which we have considered up to this point have been based on explicit statements or overt behavior on the part of our subjects. They have told us in so many words that they were or were not interested in a particular topic, or they have behaved in such a way that interest could be taken for granted.

Table 38

Those who manifest interest in labor problems through the spontaneous mention of labor as an important campaign issue are more stable in their attitudes toward labor unions than are other respondents.

(Elmira Study)

	Index Value	Number of Cases
Spontaneous mention of labor problems	.05	102
No spontaneous mention	.08	667

We can also tell something about the concerns and interests of our subjects without their doing or saying anything. We do this by inferring their attitudes from knowledge of the social groups to which they belong. As our research experience increases so does our fund of knowledge about the interests and concerns of different social groups. Over the years we have come to know, with fair exactness, what topics interest men, what issues concern women, and so on. In a study such as the present one, then, we can put this knowledge to use. Starting out with information about the social characteristics of our respondents we can infer which groups will be concerned with a particular topic and which will not. We can then determine whether those to whom we have attributed greater interest show more stable response patterns when asked related attitude questions.

It is perhaps easiest to infer interest in a question area when that area is one of immediate relevance to the respondent's social group. And, with previous results in mind, we should expect the more interested to be more stable in their responses.[8] Thus we anticipate that Jews will have the most stable attitudes on issues dealing with Jews; we expect that young people will have more consistent response patterns on questions dealing with problems of youth; and so on.

Very much along these lines is the behavior of men and women on different types of questions. As we know from a variety of studies, women are generally less interested than men in public affairs. In our data this lack of concern is reflected in greater turnover, among women, on questions dealing with these topics. In Table 39 we have collected relevant questions from the Cincinnati Study. The differences, while not always substantial, show the greater instability of women when they are interviewed on topics of this sort:

Table 39

Women, to whom we attribute little interest in public affairs, are less stable than men in their answers to questions dealing with these topics.

Question		Index Value	Number of Cases
(a) "In general, are you satisfied or dissatisfied with the progress that the United Nations Organization has made so far?"			
	Men	.15	120
	Women	.22	198
(b) "Do you think you would be better off personally if the United States would trade more with foreign countries?"			
	Men	.14	144
	Women	.20	350
(c) "As far as you know is it the job of the United Nations to deal with disarmament and the A-bomb?"			
	Men	.18	119
	Women	.22	206
(d) "Do you yourself take interest in news about our trade with other countries?"			
	Men	.10	145
	Women	.12	350

But there are special areas of activity - marketing, child care, and the like - which are usually defined as woman's domain; on questions falling within this province we expect women to feel more concerned than do men. Accordingly, we anticipate that when answers to these essentially "feminine" topics are studied, the pattern of relative stability will be reversed, with women showing less turnover than men. This is indeed the case. Although the differences are never great, they are consistent. In the Baltimore Study, for example, one of the indices of personality structure dealt, in its manifest content, with problems of child-rearing. The item read as follows: "The most important thing to teach children is absolute obedience to their parents." As Table 40 shows, married women were somewhat more consistent than married men in their agreement or disagreement with this statement:

Table 40

Married women are more stable than married men when they are asked a question about child-rearing, presumably a topic in which they take special interest.

(Baltimore Study)

Among Married Respondents Who Are:	Index Value	Number of Cases
Men	.12	171
Women	.06	225

There is a second result in the Baltimore Study similar to this last one. Another of the personality items asked the respondents whether they agreed that "Prison is too good for sex criminals; they should be publicly whipped or worse." Women, we can assume, consider themselves responsible for the welfare and safety of their families; the question of how to deal with sex criminals is therefore something of special concern to them. This reveals itself in their greater stability in answering the question. This is shown in Table 41.

Women also show somewhat greater stability on a question from the Elmira Study dealing with price controls.[9] This again is an area in which a woman's role as homemaker would presumably lead to high interest. To be sure, the question as it was worded posed the problem as a social issue, and, during the presidential campaign when it was raised, it was also a political issue. Nonetheless, we may suppose that this was one campaign issue in which women were more interested than men. At any rate, they are slightly more consistent in their responses. This is shown in Table 42.

Table 41

Women are more stable than men in their opinions as to how sex criminals should be treated, a question of special concern to them.

(Baltimore Study)

	Index Value	Number of Cases
Men	.18	187
Women	.15	248

Table 42

Women are more stable than men when they are asked a question about price controls, a campaign issue in which they take special interest.

(Elmira Study)

	Index Value	Number of Cases
Men	.07	346
Women	.05	433

This relationship between interest and stability of response is not an invariant one. In some instances we find that the *less* interested respondents are equally or even more stable than their more interested counterparts. These cases are relatively rare, however. The regularity with which we find high interest and high stability positively associated leaves little doubt that interest is a major factor making for consistent responses.

II. THE NATURE OF THE QUESTIONS

It would be an oversight to ignore the influence of the questions themselves in bringing about turnover. We know that different research techniques lead to different results; we also expect that they will bring about varying degrees of instability.

There are three such problems which interest us and for which we have some data.[10] These are:

(1) Turnover as a function of the *ambiguity* of questions.

(2) Turnover as a function of the *forcing* of opinion.

(3) Turnover as a function of *estimation.*

On the first question we have only qualitative data from the Baltimore Study. In addition to such material, we can present some statistical evidence bearing on the second and third problems.

Ambiguity of the Questions

It is important, in any study using questionnaire techniques, to make sure that the individual items are not ambiguous. If we do not know how a respondent understood a question, we cannot very easily interpret his answer.

This is an obvious requirement, and one of which most public opinion researchers are very much aware. It is a particularly urgent requirement in studies making use of repeated interviews, however, for unless ambiguities in wording are eliminated, respondents can interpret individual questions differently on different occasions, thus producing an apparent, but spurious, change in attitude.

Despite the careful pre-testing of items used in the Baltimore Study and despite the fact that the same questions had been used successfully in previous researches, it is clear that some ambiguities remained. For example, one respondent, who had first agreed and then disagreed that "In general, Jews should not be allowed to hold high political office," commented as follows in the intensive interview:

> *It depends on how high.* Of course, I wouldn't want a Jew to be president. But they do make good executives.

It was apparently the ambiguity of the key phrase, "high political office," which accounted for the inconsistent responses of this individual.[11] It seems reasonable to assume that, on one occasion, he thought of presidential office when answering the question; on the second occasion he apparently had a lower office in mind.

Other respondents had comparable difficulties with other questions used in the Baltimore Study. Another anti-Semitism item asked the respondent whether or not he agreed that "most Jews are dirty." As we learned from several intensive interviews, the word "dirty" was not consistently defined by different respondents, or by the same respondent at different times. One respondent indicated this very explicitly in his comments:

> *How do you mean dirty?* I think I disagreed before without explanation. I think that most Jews are dirty *insofar as business dealings go. As far as physical appearances, well, I'm not too much concerned with it.* I never pay too much attention to their appearance, though there are a lot of them from a certain section of the world that don't regard their physical appearance. *I suppose that phrase comes from physical appearance.* I have heard it. *But usually it refers to sharp business practices, rather than dirty appearance...*

Here once more we see how the ambiguity of an item can make it possible for a respondent with well-formulated and unchanging attitudes to give every appearance of having changed. In the present case, acceptance of the statement that "most Jews are dirty" seems to depend on what characteristic of Jews is understood by the respondent.

It should not be thought that this kind of ambiguity was confined to the anti-Semitism questions. It characterized the so-called Berkeley items as well, particularly the one which stated "Any good leader should be strict with people under him in order to gain their respect." The intensive interview reports contain several comments regarding confusion as to what area of behavior is referred to in the question. One respondent who had originally disagreed with question, and later agreed with it, explained his shift in the following fashion:

> Well, it depends whether it is politics or business (to which the question refers). If you are the boss, I would say yes, you should be strict. That doesn't necessarily mean that you have to have a whip. If you word it so that it doesn't necessarily mean politics, then it's OK. At first I thought, well, I took it for granted you mean politics.

Another respondent, similarly confused by the intent of the question, offered some professional criticism of the wording:

> I agree with that. You have to have discipline to make an organization work. You know, those questions are loaded. When you get a question like that, *the words don't mean the same things to all people*. Now, if you mean would I support a totalitarian state, well, of course not. But if you're talking about plain strict leadership, then I'm in favor of it.

The respondent might have added that the words of the question do not mean the same thing to the same subject at different times, for he originally agreed with the statement, then disagreed with it later.

In summary, an ambiguous question is double-barrelled, or perhaps even multi-barrelled, in the sense that it becomes a different question when different meanings are assigned to the ambiguous words or phrases. This introduces no problem in a study of attitude change so long as we can assume that respondents will answer in one way no matter what interpretation they give the question; for example, if they always agree that Jews should not be allowed to hold high political office, no matter what the office may be. But as we have seen, respondents will on occasion react differently to the different "barrels" of the question. When this is the case, when the respondents' acceptance or rejection of a statement depends on their interpretations of the ambiguous words or phrases in the statement, then repeated interviewing will uncover shifting responses which can be considered only spurious changes in attitude.

Forcing of Opinion

Ambiguity is a property of the questions which are asked; the manner in which they are asked also seems to play a role in producing turnover. Sometimes it seems advisable to instruct interviewers that they should push for a definite response, rather than accept a "don't know" answer. This was the case in the Baltimore Study, for it was felt that, without this procedure, many respondents would avoid giving a definite answer in order to escape taking a stand on questions which were sometimes experienced as disturbing.

When these forcing techniques were used with respondents who were not interested in the topic, however, they led to expression of pseudo-opinions. By making it hard for the respondent to express his lack of interest and his lack of definite opinion, the possibility of unstable responses was increased. And this instability expressed itself in shifting responses to the panel questions.

Some of the intensive interviewers tried to reproduce the interviewing situation which had prevailed in the formal poll interviews of the Baltimore Study. Thus they tried to elicit definite statements from otherwise reluctant subjects. The effect of this procedure is clearly demonstrated in one interview:

> (Where does your sympathy lie in the conflict between the Jews and Arabs in Palestine?) Well, I haven't any. *I don't care which one wins.* (It says here that the last time you said that the Arabs should win.) Well, what are the Arabs? They're not Jews and they're not Gentiles? Well, I don't know what they are, so I don't care which one wins. (Would you like to see the Jews lose?) *Well, you want an answer.* I'll say the Arabs. But I'll tell you the truth. *It don't make any difference.*

Note how the respondent refused to take a stand for as long as possible. He starts out by saying that he doesn't care which side wins, and if we were to ascribe to him any opinion, it would be this one of indifference. But the interviewer persists in trying to get him to choose sides. Apparently more out of courtesy than anything else, he obliges her by saying that he would like the Arabs to win. But he immediately repeats his indifference.

In other cases, similar comments were offered to explain, in retrospect, changes in answers to the different items:

> (Do you remember ever feeling differently about that?) No, I don't think I felt differently. I might have felt differently. *But last time* (at the preceding poll interview) *it was understood that there was nothing you could say but "yes" or "no"... So I might have said "yes" and let it go at that.*

The respondent who understands that he can only say "yes" or "no" has a hard time indicating lack of opinion. And, being forced to take a stand, the one that he chooses is likely to change if the interview is repeated.

In order to obtain some statistical evidence of the relationship between forcing procedures and turnover of response, the schedule dealing with decision dilemmas included two experimental questions.[12] In both of them we asked the respondents to choose between two alternatives; but, unlike the other decision problems, we gave them an opportunity to say, "don't know." If they selected this answer, however, they were then asked:

> Suppose you had to give an opinion: check below which one you would give.

The original alternatives were then repeated. In this way then we attempted to force a definite answer from those who declined at first to take a stand.

The first question asked the respondent whether he believed that, in the long run, television would have a destructive or constructive effect on American family life.[13] Those answering this question can be divided into three groups. First of all, there are those subjects who were not forced in either interview; secondly, there are the respondents who answered "don't know" on one of the interviews and were therefore forced to express an opinion on that occasion; finally, there were the respondents who answered "don't know" both times and who therefore were forced both times. Comparison of these three groups reveals that instability of responses is proportional to the amount of forcing.

Table 43

Degree of turnover is proportional to the number of times the respondent was forced to make a definite response.

	Index Value	Number of Cases
Forced on both interviews	.09	106
Forced on one interview	.06	101
Forced on neither interview	.02	330

The second experimental question, one we have already considered, asked the respondent how many men had been in the Army.[14] Here again we find that those forced in both interviews to take a definite stand show the greatest degree of turnover; those forced in neither interview exhibit the smallest degree.

Table 44

Degree of turnover is also proportional to the number of times the respondent was forced to make a cognitive discrimination.

	Index Value	Number of Cases
Forced on both interviews	.17	153
Forced on one interview	.11	91
Forced on neither interview	.06	280

Both the qualitative and the statistical evidence point to forcing techniques as one aspect of the interview situation producing unstable responses.[15]

Errors of Estimation

So far we have considered the way in which the wording of a question or the requirement that a response be obtained can lead to unstable responses. There is still another way in which the nature of the questioning procedure results in turnover. There are some types of questions which respondents dislike answering and which, therefore, interviewers dislike asking. Among these are questions concerning income, age and other information considered "private" or personal. Research organizations sometimes permit their field workers to estimate these characteristics rather than risk the rapport of the interview situation. It is entirely possible, however, that when these estimates are made they result in the kind of turnover which we have been studying.

Erroneous estimations are not easily visible in a poll, except through some criterion of internal consistency. In a panel study, however, they show up as part of the turnover of the item under consideration. If the interviewer who visits the respondent on the first occasion asks a question on income and obtains a correct answer, while the second interviewer makes an inaccurate estimate, then the individual will apparently have changed his income level during the interval between the two interviews.[16]

The Baltimore Study gives some indication of the effects of these estimations on amount of turnover. In both interviews, interviewers were permitted to make their estimates of the respondent's income, but they were asked to indicate whether the information which they recorded was the respondent's answer or their estimate. There were 82 cases in which interviewers stated that they had made an estimate of income in one or both of the interviews.

The total turnover on income, then, can be divided into two parts - one part coming from the cases where no estimation was reported (although some may have occurred), and a second part obtained from those cases in which the interviewers did make estimates. The results of this separation are recorded in Table 45.

It should not be assumed, however, that these errors are confined to the interviewing staff. The respondents themselves may be at fault. We have all of us heard warnings that informants should not be asked to make estimates which involve mental calculations. From an examination of what happens when those estimates are made, the warning seems fully justified. In the Cincinnati Study respondents were asked on both interviews to tell how much rent they paid, or, if they owned their homes, to estimate "equivalent rental value." Table 46 shows just how variable these estimates were.

Table 45

There is more turnover on the cases whose income was estimated by the interviewer.

(Baltimore Study)

	Index Value	Number of Cases
All cases	.08	499
* * * * * * * *		
Estimation on one or both interviews	.16	82
No estimation	.07	417

Table 46

Those who estimate the rental value of their homes give unstable responses.

(Cincinnati Study)

	Index Value	Number of Cases
Actual rent reported by renters	.02	184
Estimated rent reported by owners	.10	244

In other words, when the interviewer or the respondent is permitted to make estimations of factual information, errors may result. And when these errors occur on more than one occasion they lead to the same kind of instability observed in connection with attitude and opinion questions.

INDEX OF TURNOVER

There were a number of different ways in which we might have measured turnover. The index with which we have worked was considered best because it derives from a theoretical model.[1]

We start out with a scheme relating observations of the same phenomenon made at different times. Suppose, for example, that we consider the respondents' classification as Negro or White. Our data could be represented by the following four-fold table:

		Interview I		
		White	Negro	
Interview II	White	a	s	p_2
	Negro	s'	a'	q_2
		p_1	q_1	1

We know, or rather we can assume, that there are some inaccuracies in this classification. Some of the Whites are erroneously reported as Negroes, and some Negroes are mistakenly classified as Whites. In other words, if K_I is the "true" proportion of Whites and K_{II} the "true" proportion of Negroes, we know that:[2]

$$K_I \neq p_1 \neq p_2, \text{ and}$$

$$K_{II} \neq q_1 \neq q_2$$

What we want to know is the size of this error. How frequently do these misclassifications occur? In order to develop a measure of this error, to serve as our index of turnover, we must distinguish two empirical situations which may occur. First of all, we may observe in our data that the marginals are constant, that $p_1 = p_2$. Secondly, we may observe changing marginals, where $p_1 \neq p_2$. A different model is required for these two situations.

Index Value for Constant Marginals

Ideally, we should like a model which does not require that the error be the same for all groups being classified. That is, we do not want to assume that the error of classification need be the same for both Negroes and Whites. A model permitting us to avoid that restriction, however, has more parameters than can be solved for with data obtained through only two observations. Accordingly, we have had to make that assumption in developing the index of turnover.

Assuming that the probability of misclassification, (x), is the same for both Negroes and Whites, we can set up the following latent scheme:

True Proportions	Reported White in first interview	Reported White in second interview
K_I	(1-x)	(1-x)
K_{II}	x	x

From this latent structure it is a relatively easy matter to determine a value for x. We do this by stating one of our observed turnover cells in terms of latent values. (Since the marginals are assumed to be constant here, s = s', and it does not matter which we choose.)

$$s' = K_I\,(1-x)\,x + K_{II}\,x\,(1-x)$$

$$= (1-x)\,x\,(K_I + K_{II})$$

$$o = x^2 - x + s'$$

Often it is not realistic to assume that the marginals are constant. We observe a difference between p_1 and p_2. In these instances the model leading to the equation we have just derived is not applicable.

Index Value for Changing Marginals

In order to develop our new model, let us consider reports of age obtained at two times. As in the previous case, we assume a true proportion of people who are "young" at the time of the first interview. But, instead of assuming that this proportion is the same in the second interview, we consider that a percentage, C, have become older in the interval between the two interviews.[3] Thus we now have three latent classes:

$K_I(1-C)$ - those who are "truly" young at the time of both interviews

K_IC - those who change from young to old

K_{II} - those who are old at the time of both interviews

With these three classes, we can set up the following latent cross-tabulation:

		Interview I: Young	Interview I: Old	
Interview II	Young	$K_I(1-C)$	0	$K_I(1-C)$
	Old	K_IC	K_{II}	$K_IC + K_{II}$
		K_I	K_{II}	

Again, however, we assume that errors of classification are made in both interviews, so that the observed four-fold table differs from the "true" one.[4] Once more we want to find out how large this error is.

We can set up a latent scheme similar to that considered in the preceding section.

True proportions	Reported young in the first interview	Reported young in second interview
$K_I(1-C)$	$(1-x)$	$(1-x)$
K_IC	$(1-x)$	x
K_{II}	x	x

As in the previous model, we can determine the value of x if we first state some of the observed figures in latent terms.

First of all, let us consider the difference between p_1 and p_2:

$$p_1 - p_2 = K_I(1-x) + K_{II}x - K_I(1-C)\ (1-x) - K_ICx - K_{II}x.$$

$$= K_IC(1-x) - K_ICx$$

$$= K_IC(1-2x)$$

This difference will be useful in our next equation.

The second step is to express one of the turnover cells in latent terms. Since we are now dealing with changing marginals, the two turnover cells are not equal to each other. One of them, s, was empty in the latent scheme. We can expect, however, that the observed data will show a number of cases in this cell, although fewer than in the other turnover cell.

$$s = K_I(1\text{-}C)x(1\text{-}x) + K_1Cx^2 + K_{II}(1\text{-}x)x$$

$$= K_Ix(1\text{-}x) + K_{II}(1\text{-}x)x - K_ICx(1\text{-}x) + K_ICx^2$$

$$= x(1\text{-}x) - K_ICx(1\text{-}2x)$$

We saw above that $(p_1 - p_2) = K_IC(1\text{-}2x)$. Hence

$$s = x(1\text{-}x) - x(p_1\text{-}p_2)$$

$$= x(1\text{-}x\text{-}p_1 + p_2)$$

$$= x(q_1+p_2\text{-}x).$$

If we call $(q_1 + p_2)$ R, then

$$s = x(R - x)$$

$$0 = x^2 - Rx + s$$

R and s are observed data; with this information we can compute the value of x. This is the index which has been used throughout the text. It will be noted that the equation we have just derived is the general one, and the model for constant marginals a specific case. When $p_1 = p_2$, then R is 1, and we have the equation discussed earlier.

ADDITIONAL MATERIAL BEARING ON DECISION CONFLICTS

In Chapter 1 we reported a number of results in summary form. But we did not have an opportunity there to present all 18 of the decision problems on which our analysis was based, nor did we find it possible to report the results for each question separately. In this appendix, therefore, we shall present our data in more detailed form. (Some of it has already been discussed in the text, and is therefore, familiar. In order to present the complete picture, however, we shall repeat those results here.)

What we shall do is quote the various forms in which the questions appear, indicating on which schedule each was found. Then we shall report the marginal symmetry for each version of the question, the number of persons reporting little difficulty in answering the question, and, finally, the value of the turnover index. This is the complete set of data on which all of our previous analysis was based.

Question 2

AD: When we think of the ideal kind of job, most of us would probably agree that we want a secure job which is important and well-paying at the same time. But sometime during their lives many people have to choose between a *secure* job which does not and *never* will pay well and a *well-paying* job which is not and *never* will be secure.

If you were offered two jobs, *equally interesting and important*, which do you think you would choose?

- I would choose the *secure* job, even though it does not and never will pay well
- I would choose the *well-paying* job, even though it is not and never will be secure

BE: When we think of the ideal kind of job, most of us would probably agree that we want a secure job which is important and well-paying at the same time. But sometime during their lives many people have to choose between a *secure* job which would *never* be well-paying, or a well-paying job which was not secure at the time that you took it but *might* become secure in the future.

If you were offered two jobs, *equally interesting and important,* which do you think you would choose?

- I would choose the *secure* job, even though it will *never* by well-paying
- I would choose the *well-paying* job, which was not secure at the time that I took it but *might* become secure in the future

CF: When we think of the ideal kind of job, most of us would probably agree that we want a secure job, which is important and well-paying at the same time. But sometime during their lives many people have to choose between a *secure* job which is not well-paying at the time you take the job but *might* be better paid in the future, or a *well-paying* job which would *never* be secure.

If you were offered two jobs, *equally interesting and important,* which do you think you would choose?

- I would choose the *secure* job which was not well-paying at the time but *might* be better paid in the future
- I would choose the *well-paying* job which would *never* be secure

The results were as follows:

	AD	BE	CF
Symmetry of marginals[1]	46-54	20-80	77-23
Percent reporting "little difficulty"[2]	37	52	59
Index value	.06	.04	.03

Question 3

AD: Only rarely can one make outstanding contributions to the world and still have time to live a "well rounded" life. Do you think it is more desirable for a person to make outstanding contributions in his field, even if it means sacrificing a well-rounded life, or is it more desirable for a person to live a well-rounded life even if it means making no contributions to his field?

- It is more desirable to make outstanding contributions
- It is more desirable to live a well-rounded life

BE: Only rarely can one make outstanding contributions to the world and still have time to live a "carefree" life. Do you think it is more desirable for a person to work hard all his life in the hope of making some worthwhile contributions, or is it more desirable for a person to live a carefree life, working only hard enough to earn a decent living?

- It is more desirable to work hard in the hope of making some contributions
- It is more desirable to live a carefree life

CF: Only rarely can one make outstanding contributions to the world and still have time to live a "well rounded" life. Do you think it is more desirable for a person to make great achievements like Einstein, Newton or Darwin, at the price of not really living outside of his work, or is it more desirable to live a full, well-rounded life at the price of not being great?

- It is more desirable to make great achievements
- It is more desirable to live a full, well-rounded life

Here we obtained the following results:

	AD	BE	CF
Symmetry of marginals	30-70	63-37	15-85
Percent reporting "little difficulty"	43	42	64
Index value	.04	.10	.02

Question 4

AD: Sometimes we have a conflict between our ideals. For example, we might find ourselves in a situation where our belief in freedom of speech was in conflict with our feeling of wanting to preserve American institutions which are dear to us.

That might happen if you heard a speaker advocating sending all Negroes to Africa. What would you recommend be done with the man?

- Allow him to speak, even though he might influence some people to un-American behavior
- Prevent him from speaking, even though that would deprive him of his constitutional right to free speech

BE: Sometimes we have a conflict between our ideals. For example, we might find ourselves in a situation where our belief in freedom of speech was in conflict with our feeling of wanting to preserve American institutions which are dear to us.

That might happen if you heard a speaker advocating the overthrow of our government. What would you recommend be done with the man?

- Allow him to speak even though he might influence some people to un-American behavior
- Prevent him from speaking, even though that would deprive him of his constitutional right to free speech

CF: Sometimes we have a conflict between our ideals. For example, we might find ourselves in a situation where our belief in freedom of speech was in conflict with our feeling of wanting to preserve American institutions which are dear to us.

That might happen if you heard an atheist advocating the abolition of religion in this country. What would you recommend be done with the man?

- Allow him to speak even though he might influence some people to atheistic behavior
- Prevent him from speaking, even though that would deprive him of his constitutional right to free speech

Our respondents answered this question in the following way:

	AD	BE	CF
Symmetry of marginals	83-17	73-27	92-8
Percent reporting "little difficulty"	48	41	60
Index value	.08	.09	.02

Question 5

AD, BE: Suppose that you discovered that your *best friend* had stolen $100 from the school bookstore. Although everyone was very excited about the theft, your friend would probably not be caught unless *you* reported him. (Your friend would never find out who had made the report.) What do you think you probably would do?

- I would probably say and do nothing.
- I would try to persuade my friend to return the money. If he refused I would probably do nothing.
- I would try to persuade him to return the money. If he refused I would probably report him.
- I would probably report him as soon as I discovered what he had done.

CF: Suppose that you discovered that someone you *knew but did not like* had stolen $100 from the school bookstore. Although everyone was very excited about the theft, the person would probably not be caught unless you reported him. (He would never find out who had made the report.) What do you think you probably would do?

- I would probably say and do nothing.
- I would try to persuade him to return the money. If he refused I would probably do nothing.
- I would try to persuade him to return the money. If he refused I would probably report him.
- I would probably report him as soon as I discovered what he had done.

Answers to this question[3] took the following form:

	AD, BE	CF
Symmetry of marginals	65-35	39-61
Percent reporting "little difficulty"	34	39
Index value	.08	.06

Question 6

AD, BE: Suppose you discovered that someone you *know but didn't like* had knocked down another student with his car and had just kept on driving, without reporting the accident or offering to help the person he had injured. Although everyone was very excited about the accident, he probably would not be caught unless you reported him or her. (He would never find out who had made the report.) What do you think you probably would do?

- I would probably say and do nothing
- I would try to persuade him to turn himself in. If he refused, I would probably do nothing
- I would try to persuade him to turn himself in. If he refused, I would probably report him
- I would probably report him as soon as I discovered what he had done

CF: Suppose you discovered that your *best friend* had knocked down another student with his car and had just kept on driving, without reporting the accident or offering to help the person he had injured. Although everyone was very excited about the accident, your friend probably would not be caught unless *you* reported him. (Your friend would never find out who had made the report.) What do you think you probably would do?

- I would probably say and do nothing
- I would try to persuade my friend to turn himself in. If he refused, I would probably do nothing.
- I would try to persuade my friend to turn himself in. If he refused, I would probably report him
- I would probably report him as soon as I discovered what he had done

The results for this question[4] were:

	AD, BE	CF
Symmetry of marginals	21-79	50-50
Percent reporting "little difficulty"	47	39
Index value	.08	.06

Question 7

AD: The city of Baker, Oregon, requires that, if a minor under 18 breaks the law, one of his parents must pay the fine and serve his jail sentence.

A 16-year old boy, whose parents never paid much attention to his upbringing, breaks a school window. Do you think it would be fair or unfair to punish his parents?

- I think it would be *fair* to punish his parents
- I think it would be *unfair* to punish his parents

BE: The city of Baker, Oregon, requires that, if a minor under 18 breaks the law, one of his parents must pay the fine and serve his jail sentence.

A 16-year old boy breaks a school window. His parents have always worked hard to bring up a large family but could not spend much time with their children. Do you think it would be fair or unfair to punish his parents?

- I think it would be *fair* to punish his parents.
- I think it would be *unfair* to punish his parents

CF: The city of Baker, Oregon, requires that, if a minor under 18 breaks the law, one of his parents must pay the fine and serve his jail sentence.

A 16-year old boy, whose parents always tried hard to teach him right from wrong, breaks a school window. Do you think it would be fair or unfair to punish his parents?

- I think it would be *fair* to punish his parents
- I think it would be *unfair* to punish his parents

Here we obtained the following results:

	AD	BE	CF
Symmetry of marginals	78-22	24-76	20-80
Percent reporting "little difficulty"	58	49	61
Index value	.09	.08	.04

Question 8

AD: Some authorities have stated that television will have a beneficial effect on American family life. They say it tends to keep the family at home together, gives them a common experience, and increases the children's information.

Other authorities have stated that television will have harmful effects on American family life. They say that television inhibits conversation, standardizes tastes, and interferes with school work.

Do you think, in the long run, television will have *destructive* or *constructive* effects on American family life?

- A destructive influence
- A constructive influence

BE: Some authorities have stated that television will have a beneficial effect on American family life. They say it tends to keep the family at home together, gives them a common experience, and increases the children's information.

Do you think, in the long run, television will have *destructive* or *constructive* effects on American family life?

- A destructive influence
- A constructive influence

CF: Do you think, in the long run, television will have *destructive* or *constructive* effects on American family life?

- A destructive influence
- A constructive influence

Our respondents answered this question in the following way:

	AD	BE	CF
Symmetry of marginals	22-78	28-72	17-83
Percent reporting "little difficulty"	38	44	56
Index value	.03	.06	.04

Question 9

AD: A girl wants to marry her childhood sweetheart, even though her parents, who have always been very liberal with her, advise her against it. The girl has tried to persuade her parents to see her point of view, but they maintain their attitude. What do you think the girl should do?

- Follow the advice of her parents
- Marry her childhood sweetheart against the advice of her parents

BE: A girl wants to marry her childhood sweetheart, even though her parents are somewhat opposed to the marriage. The girl has tried to persuade her parents to see her point of view, but they maintain their attitude. What do you think the girl should do?

- Abide by the wishes of her parents
- Marry her childhood sweetheart, despite the parents' opposition

CF: A girl wants to marry her childhood sweetheart, even though her parents say that they will disown her if she does. The girl has tried to persuade her parents to see her point of view, but they maintain their attitude. What do you think the girl should do?

- Abide by the wishes of her parents
- Marry her childhood sweetheart, despite her parents' opposition

Here the results were:

	AD	BE	CF
Symmetry of marginals	36-64	11-89	10-90
Percent reporting "little difficulty"	36	45	51
Index value	.08	.02	.01

Question 11

D: Suppose two people asked you to room with them next year. One of them was a very popular student and a lot of fun to be with. The other was a fairly shy person who didn't know too many other students and might therefore have a hard time finding another room-mate.

With whom do you think you would room?

- The popular student
- The fairly shy student

E: Suppose two people asked you to room with them next year. One of them was a very popular student and a lot of fun to be with. The other was a person whom you considered uninteresting but who liked you a lot.

With whom do you think you would room?

- The popular student
- The uninteresting student

F: Suppose two people asked you to room with them next year. One of them was a very popular student and a lot of fun to be with. The other was an extremely shy person who depended on you a good deal and who undoubtedly would be very lonely if you roomed with someone else.

With whom do you think you would room?

- The popular student
- The very shy student

The results of this question were:

	D	E	F
Symmetry of marginals	62-38	66-34	51-49
Percent reporting "little difficulty"	33	25	33
Index value	.04	.04	.06

Question 12

AD: Suppose that you had planned to stay home one particular evening to catch up on past reading assignments. In the late afternoon you learn that two very good friends of yours have announced their engagement and that there will be a big party for them that evening. What do you think you probably would do?

- Stay home and read
- Go to the party

BE: Suppose that you had planned to stay home one particular evening to study for a tough final examination to be given the following day. In the late afternoon you learn that two very good friends of yours have announced their engagement and that there will be a big party for them that evening. What do you think you probably would do?

- Stay home and study
- Go to the party

CF: Suppose that you had planned to stay home one particular evening to work on a difficult term paper due a week later. In the late afternoon you learn that two very good friends of yours have announced their engagement and that there will be a big party for them that evening. What do you think you probably would do?

- Stay home and work on the paper
- Go to the party

We obtained the following results:

	AD	BE	CF
Symmetry of marginals	8-92	52-48	20-80
Percent reporting "little difficulty"	57	35	58
Index value	.03	.13	.04

Question 13

AD: Because the number of courses we can take is limited, most of us, at one time or another, are faced with the following dilemma in planning our programs. We sometimes have to choose between a dull course, which is very important for our field of study, and an extremely interesting course not related to our field. If you had to make that choice, what do you think you would do?

- Choose the dull course important for my field of study
- Choose the extremely interesting course not related to my field of study

BE: Because the number of courses we can take is limited, most of us, at one time or another, are faced with the following dilemma in planning our program. We sometimes have to choose between a dull course which is very important for our field of study, and a more interesting course not related to our field. If you had to make that choice, what do you think you would do?

- Choose the dull course important for my field of study
- Choose the more interesting course not related to my field of study

CF: Because the number of courses we can take is limited, most of us, at one time or another, are faced with the following dilemma in planning our program. We sometimes have to choose between a dull course which is very important for our field of study, and an interesting course which is quite possibly not so valuable. If you had to make that choice, what do you think you would do?

- Choose the dull course important for my field of study
- Choose the more interesting course possibly not so valuable to my field of study

The results of this question were as follows:

	AD	BE	CF
Symmetry of marginals	82-18	83-17	79-21
Percent reporting "little difficulty"	48	50	57
Index value	.03	.08	.06

Question 14

AD: Suppose you were taking a final examination, and your fiance, who was sitting next to you, asked you for the answer to one of the questions. There was some chance of being caught, but it seemed that you could probably give the information safely.

However, if you were caught it would mean, at the very least, that you would fail the course. What would you do?

- Act as though I hadn't received the note and ignore my fiance
- Whisper a few key words and hope that he (she) will understand them
- Pass the complete answer to the question, even though there is a greater chance of being caught

BE: Suppose you were taking a final examination, and an acquaintance, who was sitting next to you, asked you for the answer to one of the questions. There was some chance of being caught, but it seemed that you could probably give the information safely. *However, if you were caught, it would mean, at the very least, that you would fail the course.* What would you do?

- Act as though I hadn't received the note and ignore him (her)
- Whisper a few key words and hope that he (she) will understand them
- Pass the complete answer to the question, even though there is a greater chance of being caught

CF: Suppose you were taking a final examination and your best friend, who was sitting next to you, asked you for the answer to one of the questions. There was some chance of being caught, but it seemed that you could probably give the information safely. *However, if you were caught, it would mean, at the very least, that you would fail the course.* What would you do?

- Act as though I hadn't received the note and ignore my friend
- Whisper a few key words and hope that my friend will be able to understand them
- Pass the complete answer to the question, even though there is a greater chance of being caught

Answers to this question[5] were as follows:

	AD	BE	CF
Symmetry of marginals	31-69	55-45	42-58
Percent reporting "little difficulty"	27	37	36
Index value	.07	.09	.06

Question 25

When you are reading for pleasure, and not for school work, what kind of book do you generally prefer, fiction or non-fiction?

- Fiction
- Non-fiction

This question, which appeared in one form only, elicited the following kinds of responses:

Symmetry of marginals	57-43
Percent reporting "little difficulty"	63
Index value	.08

Question 26

Would you say that, all things being equal, you would prefer to see a war-movie or a comedy on the screen?

- War-movie
- Comedy

This question also was only asked in one form. The results were as follows:

Symmetry of marginals	19-81
Percent reporting "little difficulty"	64
Index value	.05

Question 27

If you had your choice, would you prefer to spend your vacation at the seashore or in the mountains?

- At the seashore
- In the mountains

The results of this question, again asked in one form only, were as follows:

Symmetry of marginals	56-44
Percent reporting "little difficulty"	58
Index value	.06

Question 29

AD: At the height of the war, how many men were there in the United States Army, 7,000,000 or 3,000,000?

- 7,000,000
- 3,000,000

BE: At the height of the war, how many men were there in the United States Army, 7,000,000 or 25,000,000?

- 7,000,000
- 25,000,000

CF: At the height of the war, how many men were there in the United States Army, 6,000,000 or 7,000,000?

- 6,000,000
- 7,000,000

The results were as follows:[6]

	AD	BE	CF
Symmetry of marginals	84-16	71-29	33-67
Index value	.08	.06	.15

Question 30

AD: When was the Battle of Gettysburg fought, July 1863, or September 1863?

- July 1863
- September 1863

BE: When was the Battle of Gettysburg fought, 1863 or 1864?

- 1863
- 1864

CF: When was the Battle of Gettysburg fought, 1812 or 1863?

- 1812
- 1863

Here we obtained the following results:

	AD	BE	CF
Symmetry of marginals	58-42	55-45	13-87
Index value	.22	.14	.02

Question 36

AD: What is the correct title of Charles Darwin's great work: "The Origin of Species" or "The Meaning of Relativity"?

- "The Origin of Species"
- "The Meaning of Relativity"

BE: What is the title of Charles Darwin's great work: "The Origin of Species" or "The Origin of the Species"?

- "The Origin of Species"
- "The Origin of the Species"

CF: What is the correct title of Charles Darwin's great work: "The Origin of Species" or 'Up from the Apes?"

- "The Origin of Species"
- 'Up From the Apes"

The results of this final question were:

	AD	BE	CF
Symmetry of marginals	90-10	51-49	91-9
Index value	.05	.11	.03

QUESTIONS USED IN STUDYING THE INFLUENCE OF MOOD

In Chapter 2, we indicated that there were 14 attitude questions which were used in studying the relationship between attitude and mood changes. In this appendix we shall report both the wording of these questions, and the distribution of responses in both interviews.

Question 13: On the whole, how satisfied are you with this school?

	Int. I	Int. II
Very satisfied	21%	22%
Quite satisfied	48	50
Somewhat or very dissatisfied	31	28
	504	504

Question 14: How well do you think your school is preparing you for the work you intend to do after college?

	Int. I	Int. II
Very well	25%	22%
Fairly well	55	56
Not so well or not at all well	20	22
	495	495

Question 15: In general, about how interested are your teachers in their students?

	Int. I	Int. II
Extremely interested	7%	6%
Quite interested	49	55
Only somewhat or slightly interested	44	39
	502	502

Question 17: At the present moment, what are your feelings about the progress you are making in your studies?

	Int. I	Int. II
At the present time, I'm completely satisfied with the progress I'm making	10%	8%
At the present time, I'm doing satisfactory work, but I would like to do better	78	78
I'm passing, or I'm not sure I'm passing my courses	12	14
	505	505

Question 18: On the whole, do you think that you worry about your school work more than other students, less than others, or about the same?

	Int. I	Int. II
I worry more than others	31%	29%
I worry about the same as others	49	52
I worry less than others	20	19
	506	506

Question 19: Generally, do you think you get a better break, not as good, or about the same break from your professors compared to other students whom you know?

	Int. I	Int. II
I get a better break	7%	7%
I get about the same break	87	85
I don't get as good a break	6	8
	505	505

Question 20: Would you say that there are some kinds of students who make themselves obnoxious?

	Int. I	Int. II
No, none that I can think of	18%	21%
Yes	82	79
	503	503

Question 21: How would you describe students who get only A's in their courses?

	Int. I	Int. II
In my experience, they are generally not as nice as students who get less good marks	9%	7%
They seem to me the same as any other students, except that they get better marks	83	86
In my experience, they're generally nicer than students who get less good marks	8	7
	496	496

Question 22: Do you think that the professors give you the benefit of the doubt when marking your papers and examinations?

	Int. I	Int. II
All or most of the time	34%	36%
Some of the time	44	44
Once in a while or never	22	20
	499	499

Question 23: In general, to what extent do your teachers encourage classroom discussion?

	Int. I	Int. II
There is *a lot* of encouragement of classroom discussion	22%	10%
There is *quite a bit* of encouragement of classroom discussion	40	43
There is some or little encouragement of classroom discussion	38	47
	497	497

Question 24: When you are called on in class, do you feel self-conscious, or are you at ease?

	Int. I	Int. II
I feel very self-conscious	11%	9%
I feel somewhat self-conscious	37	38
I feel pretty much or completely at ease	52	53
	497	497

Question 25: In general, how would you rate the teaching ability of your professors?

	Int. I	Int. II
On the whole my teachers have a great deal of ability	25%	22%
On the whole my teachers are very able, but there is some room for improvement	62	65
On the whole my professors are only fair, or they do not have much ability	13	13
	501	501

Question 26: How often do you have the feeling that you would like to "tell off" the professors with whom you work most closely?

	Int. I	Int. II
I never have that feeling	25%	21%
I seldom have that feeling	45	51
I sometimes or usually have that feeling	30	28
	508	508

Question 27: If you had it to do over again, would you come to this school or would you go to some other school?

	Int. I	Int. II
I would definitely come to this school	28%	27%
I would probably come to this school	44	48
I would probably or definitely go someplace else	28	25
	505	505

On all but one of these questions, the marginal distributions for the total sample remained constant from one interview to the next.[1] But within the different mood classes this constancy is no longer observed. There is generally a reflection of mood changes in the distribution of responses given in the two interviews:

Table 47

There is generally a tendency for attitude change on the 14 questions to parallel mood change.

	Percent in Each Mood Class Giving Positive Responses[2]							
	(+ +)		(+ -)		(- +)		(- -)	
	Int. I	Int. II	Int. I	Int. II	Int. I	Int. II	Int. I	Int. II
Satisfaction with school	67	75	76	74	75	77	59	63
Satisfaction with preparation for later work	82	81	85	80	79	77	71	69
Interest of teachers	59	65	61	61	48	62	54	55
Feelings about progress of studies	90	87	89	84	86	88	86	85
Worry about school work	73	80	70	67	71	73	61	63
Feelings about breaks	92	91	94	91	94	95	94	94
Obnoxious students	23	23	13	22	17	22	16	16
Students who get only A's	92	95	89	90	91	93	92	94
Getting benefit of doubt	81	83	78	78	72	76	79	79
Encouragement of discussion	61	59	68	52	55	43	61	53
Self-consciousness	55	57	47	49	52	57	52	49
Teaching ability of professors	89	88	85	87	89	88	87	85
"Telling off" professors	73	74	70	67	68	77	69	70
Return to present school	76	78	77	74	69	75	65	73
Average for all questions	72.4	74.0	78.7	69.8	69.0	78.8	67.6	67.7

The parallel between mood and attitude change is not always consistent in these individual questions. We recall, however, that there were three additional items which, in their wording, stressed mood more. Here the parallel is very close. Before showing this, let us report the exact questions.

Question 5: Sometimes people behave differently according to their mood. We would like you to tell us what you think you would do, feeling as you do today, if you found yourself in any one of the following situations:

(a) Suppose that you had a lunch date with a very close friend, who was late and kept you waiting for a long time.

If I felt the way I feel today, I would

	Int. I	Int. II
Leave the restaurant and when I see my friend tell him in no uncertain terms what I think of people who are late for appointments	1%	3%
Leave the restaurant and later inquire what had kept my friend from being on time	19	29
Just wait getting madder and madder	25	15
Just wait calmy until it seemed clear that my friend would not show up	55	53
	427	427

(b) Suppose you and a friend were standing in line waiting to get into a movie and noticed that a couple had sneaked in ahead of you.

If I felt the way I feel today, I would

	Int. I	Int. II
Just ignore the couple and continue to wait in line	62%	60%
Speak politely to the couple about their unsocial behavior and suggest that they go to the end of the line where they belong	20	22
I would tell my friend loud enough for them to hear what I thought of people like that	17	16
I would make an issue of it and try to make the people move to the end of the line where they belong	1	2
	465	465

(c) Suppose that you were in a crowded subway and were continuously jostled by a woman carrying a lot of bundles.

If I felt the way I feel at the present moment, I would

	Int. I	Int. II
Tell the woman that the subway is not meant to be a moving van	-	1%
Tell the woman to be more careful	8%	13
Glare meaningfully at her	21	17
Move to another part of the subway	71	69
	407	407

Table 48 shows that, on each of these questions, there was a close parallel between mood shifts and changes in reaction to these various situations:

Table 48

There is a strong tendency for mood shifts to be reflected in changing reactions to annoying situations

	Percent in Each Mood Class Giving Unaggressive Reactions							
	(+ +)		(+ -)		(- +)		(- -)	
	Int. I	Int. II	Int. I	Int. II	Int. I	Int. II	Int. I	Int. II
Waiting for date	71	68	58	37	46	69	40	34
Waiting for movie	68	67	70	53	50	63	58	57
Travelling in subway	82	75	71	54	64	78	63	66
Average	73.7	70.0	66.3	48.0	53.3	70.0	53.7	52.3

Here the parallel is apparent, not only for the average of all questions, but also for the individual questions as well.

APPENDIX D

ERRORS OF IDENTIFICATION

To assure respondents of their anonymity, interviewers are sometimes instructed to tell them that their names will not be obtained or used in the analysis of the survey results. This procedure has the distinct advantage of decreasing motivations to give dishonest or evasive answers, a real problem in some kinds of attitude studies. But it also has the disadvantage that further contacts with the same respondents depend on our success in matching certain demographic characteristics such as age, occupation, relationship to head of house, and so on. The opportunities for lack of success in this respect are obvious. It is entirely possible that even the most honest and conscientious interviewer will mistakenly select the wrong person in a large household, particularly since there is always some confusion about exact ages, relationship to head of house, and the like.

These cases of mistaken identity are a serious enough matter in polling studies making use of area sampling techniques, for the adequacy of the sample requires that those individuals randomly selected from the enumeration lists actually are included in the sample. In panel studies, however, such mistakes introduce the possibility that *different*, rather than the same, individuals serve as respondents in the different interviews. If this is actually the case, then some of the turnover which now seems ununderstandable can be easily explained as the conflicting information about different respondents, rather than the shifting responses of the same one.

The possibility that mistakes of this kind were made was studied in both the Cincinnati and Baltimore Studies.[1] During the fieldwork phases of the Baltimore Study there was no systematic effort to find these errors. Interviewers were instructed to make a note if, during the second interview, the respondent denied having been interviewed previously.[2] In addition, the field supervisor examined each pair of schedules, supposedly obtained from the same respondent, to determine if there were any obvious errors. The pressures of the field work, however, prevented this from being a systematic examination.

Once the interviewing had been completed, all 556 of the panel cases were carefully scrutinized to see how closely the background information obtained in the first interview corresponded to that obtained in the second. Some of this information, namely age, sex, occupation and relationship to head of house, had been given the second interviewer as a means of locating the correct respondent for the interview. But there was additional background information, obtained in both interviews, which had not been given the interviewer. This included data on the religion of the respondent, his educational level, his income, his political sympathies in the 1944 presidential election, his country of birth, and his marital status.

Particular attention was paid to cases in which there were either large discrepancies on one or two items (as, for example, a shift from one end of the educational scale to the other), or small discrepancies on many questions. These procedures are admittedly impressionistic and somewhat arbitrary. Nonetheless, as a result of them, we were able to isolate 53 cases, approximately 10 percent of the total originally obtained, in which it seemed extremely doubtful that the same person had served as the respondent in both interviews.

In some instances it was relatively easy to visualize how the mistakes came about. For example, one panel case was obtained in a rooming house providing living quarters for transient dockworkers.[3] It is altogether possible that the man interviewed in November had moved away by May, when the second interview took place. There was ample evidence, in any case, that two different persons had been interviewed:

	First Interview	Second Interview
Birthplace:	Russia	Poland
Marital status:	Wife in Europe	Never married
Vote in 1944:	Roosevelt	Don't remember

There are always similarities in the records of the two interviews which make it impossible to be absolutely certain that a mistake in identification has occurred. For example, in the present case, religious affiliation and education were the same in both interviews. These similarities are not inconsistent with the theory that two respondents were interviewed, for we expect people living in the same neighborhood to have certain socio-economic and cultural characteristics in common. But the similarities make it difficult to be sure of errors of identification.

In other cases, however, certain as we are that some mistake occurred, and that different people were interviewed, it is not so immediately obvious how this happened. In the most clearcut case, where even the address written on the two schedules is different (the house number on one is "2115" and on the other "2119"), we find the following discrepancies in background information:

	First Interview	Second Interview
Religion:	Catholic	Protestant
Education:	Complete high school	Some grade school
Age:*	45-54	55-64
Vote in 1944:	Roosevelt	Dewey
Income:*	$110-129/week	$70-$89/week
Number in household:	Five	Three

*These changes in age and income are, of course, possible.

Interestingly enough, the same occupation is recorded on both schedules. Since the occupation information obtained in the first interview was given to the second interviewer, however, it may be that he wrote it in without asking the second respondent.

We shall see presently how the exclusion of these 53 cases affects the results of the Baltimore Study.

The Cincinnati Study made use of somewhat different techniques for locating cases of mistaken identification. First of all, the interviewers conducting the reinterviews were asked to give their impressions, supported by whatever evidence they had, as to whether the respondent had been previously questioned. The results are summarized in Table 49:

Table 49

Most interviewers believe the respondents they visited had definitely been interviewed before.

(Cincinnati Study)

	Percent
Almost positively interviewed before -- no further comment	74%
Almost posivitely interviewed before -- interviewer remembers respondent	3
Almost positively interviewed before -- respondent referred to previous interview .	16
Almost positively interviewed before -- the factual data matched so well	2
Some possibility not interviewed before -- no further comments	1
Some possibility not interviewed before -- does not match description	1
Some possibility not interviewed before . . .	3
Total cases	591

According to the impressions of the interviewers then, there was doubt in only 5 percent of the cases.

In addition to this impressionistic appraisal, efforts were made to detect errors in identification by matching the name of the last school attended. The results of this are shown in Table 50:

Table 50

In most cases the name of the last school attended was the same on both schedules.

(Cincinnati Study)

	Percent
Last school attended *different* on two ballots	11%
Last school attended *same* on both ballots	77
Data incomplete	12
Total cases	585

The techniques used in the Cincinnati Study to locate mistakes in identification seem somewhat less satisfactory than those used in the Baltimore Study. First of all, as we can see in Table 49, the interviewers most frequently just state their conviction that the respondent whom they interviewed had been questioned previously, without providing any supporting evidence. The interviewers may feel under some compulsion to state that the persons whom they interviewed were "almost positively interviewed before," as they may believe that their ratings as efficient interviewers, and, indeed their continuation on the interviewing staff, depend partly on their ability to locate the respondent assigned to them, We find, for example, that 80 percent of the cases later rejected as "doubtfuls" because the names of the last school attended did not correspond on the two ballots, were classified by the interviewers as being almost positively interviewed before. (As we shall see in the following paragraphs, the school name test does not seem to be completely accurate in all cases. But it does seem to detect mistakes in identification more effectively than do the interviewer ratings.)

Since the interviewers rarely provide any data which can be used to decide whether both interviews were obtained from the same respondent, that decision is usually reached after studying whether the last school attended is the same in both interviews. But this does not seem to be an infallible criterion. Members of the same family, or even residents of the same neighborhood, may have attended the same school. Using this as the sole index of correct identification, then, means that we will overlook some cases in which errors of identification have occurred.[4]

Apparently the opposite kind of error can also occur. In some cases, both interviews seem to have been obtained from the same respondent, in spite of the fact that the name of the last school attended is different on the two ballots. For example, one respondent named "Woodward High" as the last school he had attended in the first interview, and "DC" in the second. But in both interviews he listed, by name, a large number of clubs and organizations in which he claimed membership. Furthermore, the phrasing of his answers to many of the questions was so alike in both interviews that it is almost inconceivable that it was not the same person.[5] There are a number of cases of this kind in the Cincinnati Sample.

The importance of being able to locate and eliminate these doubtful cases becomes obvious when we consider the effects of including them in our panel analysis. When they are not eliminated, there is invariably more turnover on factual items than there is otherwise. Table 51 shows the extent of this effect for some of the factual material in the Baltimore Study.

Table 51

There is less turnover on factual items when the doubtful cases are eliminated.

(Baltimore Study)

	Index Value	
	Total Cases	Doubtful Cases Eliminated
	(N=556)	(N=503)
Education	.08	.05
Income	.09	.08
Religion	.02	.01
1944 Vote	.02	.01
Marital status	.03	.02

The elimination of the doubtful cases thus reduces the turnover for all items.

But even more important than being able to locate these mistakes in identification once they have occurred is a method for avoiding them before they take place. Any kind of error is considered a challenge by the researcher. But he does not feel so urgent a need to eliminate them if they have occurred at random, for they can then be handled with existing statistical techniques. It is only when the mistakes are non-random that they introduce systematic biases into our data. And mistakes in identification do not occur at random, but instead tend to be clustered in the lower socio-economic strata:

Table 52

There are more mistakes in identification on lower socio-economic levels

(Cincinnati Study)

Economic Level	Proportion of Doubtful Cases*
A and B	10%
C	13
D	21
Education	
Some or complete college	6%
Complete high school	13
Some high school	13
Complete grade school	14
Some grade school	20
Race	
White	12%
Negro	31

*Doubtful cases are those in which the interviewer indicated a possibility that the respondent had not been previously interviewed or in which the name of the last school attended was not the same on both ballots. There were 81 such cases in all.

We need not look too far for an explanation as to why errors of identification occur more frequently in the lower socio-economic levels. It may be, for instance, that the usual interviewer is more careless when working in poorer neighborhoods or households. The average interviewer, generally a woman of middle-class background, dislikes to interview in low income areas, partly because she feels ill at ease in such physical surroundings and partly because she finds it difficult to communicate with her potential respondents.[6] Their lower educational level, the greater frequency of foreign born persons who present language difficulties, their inability to understand the objectives of the interview or suspicions regarding the motives of the interviewer, all of these factors combine to make the task of interviewing in low income areas a particularly difficult one. Under these conditions the interviewer is likely to exhibit more carelessness than she would otherwise. The errors which are introduced as a result of this laxity can be eliminated only through the careful selection, training and supervision of the field staff.

But there is possibly a further reason why the errors in identification tend to be clustered in the low income groups. Although we cannot demonstrate it with the data at hand, we know from other investigations that the lower the socio-economic level, the higher the proportion of large families. When sent to a household with many adult members, even the most reliable and responsible interviewer may mistakenly select the wrong person.

What is needed, then, in addition to improved methods of field supervision is an improved system for identifying the respondents. It has been suggested facetiously that the only way to make certain that one does not mistakenly interview the wrong person is to obtain his fingerprints during the first interview and match them before conducting a second. This may be the case, for even when the name of the respondent is known, mistakes in identification can occur.[7] But it may be possible to reduce these mistakes without either knowing the name of the subject or obtaining his fingerprints. In order to do so, we need identifying information which is highly sensitive in distinguishing between individuals. Characteristics which would be common to a family or neighborhood would not serve our purposes. Religion, for example, would not be a good identifying characteristic, because all members of any one family, or even of any one neighborhhod, generally have the same religion. For the same reason, voting behavior, or nativity will be of little help. Descriptions of the physical appearance of the respondent may be of some assistance, except that coloring and physique are likely to be family, rather than individual, traits, and it may be difficult to develop standardized instructions for the description of details other than these.

Assuming that it is deemed inadvisable to identify respondents by name, the ideal information would be one or another kind of numerical designation which cannot be, or is unlikely to be, shared by more than one individual. One of the difficulties with the kind of characteristic which has been used thus far is that it divides people into different qualitative catergories, such as Protestant or Catholic. Obviously many people share these traits. Characteristics involving numerical designation are usually not so easily duplicated. Consider the following:

Exact date of birth
Social Security number
Serial number on driver's license

All of these characteristics have the advantage of being highly idiosyncratic. It is unlikely that two people in the same family will have exactly the same birthdates. (We are disregarding the possibility of having to pick one of a pair of twins.) Social Security numbers and the serial numbers of drivers' licenses are never duplicated. The chief disadvantage of using this kind of information for identification purposes, however, is that the respondents may resist supplying the necessary facts. They may feel that their privacy is invaded or their anonymity threatened if such information is recorded on their interviews. Furthermore, not everyone has a social security number or a driver's license, so that, in such cases, substitute information would have to be obtained. In spite of these difficulties some better means of locating the same person on different occasions will have to be developed. To do so will probably require considerable experimentation to determine which types of information are both infallible (to the extent that any information is infallible) and easily obtainable.

NOTES

INTRODUCTION

1. A fairly elaborate description will be found in P.F. Lazarsfeld, B. Berelson and H. Gaudet, *The People's Choice* (New York: Columbia University Press, 1948, 2nd ed.) Introduction. See also P.F. Lazarsfeld, "The Use of Panels in Social Research," *Proceedings of the American Philosophical Society* (1948), 92, 405-410.
2. This actually was the case during World War II. See S.A. Stouffer et. al., *The American Soldier*. Studies in the Social Psychology of World War II. (Princeton, New Jersey: Princeton University Press, 1949.) Vol. I, p. 265.
3. For a bibliography covering the most recent studies, see A. Anastasi and J.P. Foley, Jr., *Differential Psychology* (New York: The Macmillan Company, 1949), pp. 367-372.
4. L.M. Terman et al., *Genetic Studies of Genius*. See especially Volume III, "Followup Studies of a Thousand Gifted Children" (Stanford, Calif.: Stanford University Press, 1930); Volume IV, "The Gifted Child Grows Up" (Stanford, Calif.: Stanford University Press, 1947): and Chapter XX in Volume I, "The Mental and Physical Traits of a Thousand Gifted Children" (Stanford, Calif.: Stanford University Press, 1925).
5. Sheldon and Eleanor Glueck, *Later Criminal Careers* (New York: The Commonwealth Fund, 1937); see also the same authors, *500 Criminal Careers* (New York: Alfred A. Knopf, 1930).
6. Lazarsfeld, Berelson and Gaudet, *op. cit.*
7. T. Newcomb, *Personality and Social Change* (New York: Dryden Press, 1943).
8. It may be that a panel study covering as long a period as this one can be successful only when its subjects are members of some stable group, such as a college or the Army. Otherwise the analyst cannot be certain that it will be possible to repeat his observations.

9. Here we indicate for the first time that the repeated observations of which we talk can take the form of answers to interview *questions* which are repeated on two or more occasions. We have used the word "observation" in a rather loose way; we mean by it any kind of information about the unit under study which can be obtained, in comparable form, at successive points in time. This information can be reports of observed behavior, in the more restricted sense of the word. But the repeated observations can take other forms as well. It is conceivable, for example, that a panel study is based on documentary materials. In medical research the repeated observations are results of varied medical tests. In point of fact, however, most studies making use of repeated observations have obtained their data through schedules. The "observations" are therefore the answers to particular questions of opinion and fact.
10. This investigation, which we have called the Elmira Study, is described below.
11. *Op. cit.*
12. We also find changes in answers to questions about invariant characteristics. See Appendix D for evidence of this.
13. T.W. Adorno, E. Frenkel-Brunswik, D.J. Levinson and R.N. Sanford, *The Authoritarian Personality* (New York: Harper and Brothers, 1950.)
14. The Baltimore Study. This is described in some detail on pp. 8-9 below.
15. We do not claim that a single item such as this one can serve as a measure of basic personality traits. Several such questions were included in the Baltimore Study. We observe the same result in connection with each of them individually, and also in connection with a scale formed by combining them.
16. Consider, for example, the statement by Robert L. Thorndike: "Reliability or the consistency in a measurement procedure is a matter of degree and not an all-or-none matter. Whenever we measure anything, whether in the physical, the biological, or the social sciences, that measurement contains a certain amount of chance error. The amount of chance error may be large or small, but it is always present to some extent. If the chance errors are small in size, relative to the variation from person to person, the reliability or consistency of the

measure is high. If the chance errors become large in proportion to the variation from person to person, the reliability of the measure is low." (*Personnel Selection: Test and Measurement Techniques*. New York: John Wiley and Sons, 1949, pp. 68-69.)

17. Our study has drawn on two sources of support. The Bureau of Applied Social Research received a grant to study the theory and application of panel techniques. (The grant was made by the Committee on Measurement of Opinion, Attitudes, and Consumer Wants, set up by the National Research Council, with funds from the Rockefeller Foundation.) Access to the Bureau's materials made possible the analysis of existing panel studies from our special point of view. Secondly, Mr. Dean Manheimer and the present author received a grant from the Rockefeller Foundation to carry out experiments, some of which will be reported in this monograph.
18. In a sense the reanalysis of these existing studies takes the place of references to previous work in the field. The reader will find few bibliographical references in our manuscript. By and large this is not an oversight. Although we may accidentally have overlooked some relevant studies, it is our impression that very little has been done previously which is of direct relevance to the problems which we are studying.
19. The list of sponsors included Chicago, Columbia, Cornell and Harvard Universities, and a number of organizations, among them Elmo Roper, International Public Opinion Research, General Motors, Time, Inc., and the Anti-Defamation League.
20. The main findings are reported in an article by Shirley A. Star and Helen Mac Gill Hughes, "Report on an Educational Campaign: the Cincinnati Plan for the United Nations," *American Journal of Sociology* (1950), LV, 389-400.
21. This study was carried out by the Department of Scientific Research of the American Jewish Committee with the cooperation of the Bureau.
22. See T. W. Adorno, E. Frenkel-Brunswik, D. J. Levinson, and R. N. Sanford, *op. cit.*
23. Another phase of our research, which will not be reported here, focused on certain technical problems. Before undertaking the intensive study of conflict and mood, we wanted to make certain that various extraneous factors -- such as the time lapse between

test and retest, the anonymity or non-anonymity of subjects, and their expectations of a retest — would not affect our results. Accordingly, we conducted some preliminary experiments. None of these factors seems to have any relation to the kind or consistency of answers to our questions.

24. I wish to acknowledge my indebtedness to Mr. Dean Manheimer, my co-worker in this project. In our many joint discussions his suggestions concerning the content and form of the schedules were always most helpful. He has assumed responsibility for the analysis of other phases of these questionnaires.
25. This was not a problem in the major panel studies described earlier. In all of those, field workers visited the homes of a representative sample of people and later revisited them. The limited resources at our disposal made field work impossible.
26. Students receiving the conflict questionnaires were told that they were participating in a study of "student values and attitudes." Those answering the mood schedule were told that the study dealt with "how people felt about certain things." Even though it was more difficult to disguise the content of the mood questionnaire, no mention was made of mood changes or attitude changes.
27. The first and second forms for each individual were matched on the basis of handwriting as well as certain background information, such as exact birthdate, father's occupation, and the like. This was relatively easy, since the schedules were returned for each class separately, usually not more than 30 at a time. In only a few cases was there any question whether or not two schedules could really be attributed to the same person. When questions of this kind arose, both schedules were eliminated from the sample. There were a number of cases which could not be matched because, apparently, the respondent had been absent from class at the time the other schedule was administered. These cases were easily detected, however.
28. The index is derived in Appendix A.
29. Because the sampling distribution of the index has not yet been worked out, it is not possible to determine when one value is significantly different from another. What we have done instead is to make use of a technique which has gained acceptance in recent years. When we compared the relative stability in

two tables, we first of all made a somewhat arbitrary and impressionistic judgment as to which had a greater degree of turnover, based on the difference between the two index values. We then accumulated a large number of such comparisons and noted the frequency with which tables characterized in one way had greater turnover than those characterized in some other way. In other words, our results are based generally on the *consistency* of a variety of differences, some of them large and others of them small, rather than on the significance of any one difference. For other examples of this kind, see Stouffer et al., *op. cit.* Vol. I, p. 157.

30. See Chapter 1.
31. See Chapter 2.

CHAPTER I.

1. The question read, "Do you expect the United States to fight in another war within the next ten years?"
2. At the time that the Cincinnati Study was carried out, in September 1947 and March 1948, this alternative might have seemed more realistic than it does today.
3. The exact wording of this question was: "Do you think there should eventually be some sort of international control of A-bombs, or should each country remain free to make its own?"
4. See, for example, Edward A. Suchman, "The Intensity Component in Attitude and Opinion Research," in S.A. Stouffer, et al., *Measurement and Prediction,* Studies in Social Psychology in World War II, Volume 4. (Princeton, New Jersey: Princeton University Press, 1950).
5. This fact is documented in the principal analysis of the Elmira materials. For a recent discussion of reference group theory, see R. K. Merton and A. S. Kitt, "Contributions to the Theory of Reference Group Behavior," in *Continuities in Social Research* (eds., R. K. Merton and P. F. Lazarsfeld) Glencoe, Illinois.: The Free Press, 1950.
6. See Lazarsfeld, Berelson and Gaudet, *op. cit.,* Ch. VI, "Time of Final Decision."
7. Vote intention was dichotomized in the following way: those with a definite vote intention were in one category; those who said they didn't know which candidate to support or that they didn't intend to vote were placed in the second category.

8. The Republican voters were still less stable than the Democrats, however, despite their generally higher education. One possible explanation for this is that, when asked in juxtaposition to questions about the conduct of the war, a question on domestic policy acquires certain overtones of a loyalty test.
9. This same proposition appears, under somewhat different guise, in both economics and psychology. In studies of economic demand we encounter it in the concept of "indifference," a state of equilibrium in which the prospective consumer finds alternative combinations of commodities equally desirable and hence interchangeable. He is "indifferent" as to which combination he receives, and therefore cannot choose between them. The same notion is met, in slightly different form, in psycho-physics. The well-known Weber-Fechtner law deals with the difficulties of discriminating between objects which weigh very nearly the same amount. By generalization the law has also been found applicable to other sensory discriminations.
10. Two different kinds of wavering can be distinguished. There is, first of all, that experienced by the individual when asked, at any time, to choose between equivalent alternatives; *before* stating his choice, he alternates from one to the other. The second kind of wavering is that observed over a longer period of time; on one occasion the individual selects one alternative, on another occasion he selects the second. It is this latter which interests us especially.
11. For a definition of intervening variables, see Patricia L. Kendall and Paul F. Lazarsfeld, "Problems of Survey Analysis," in *Continuities in Social Research* (eds., R.K. Merton and P.F. Lazarsfeld. Glencoe, Ill. The Free Press, 1950) pp. 154-158.
12. Because all of the subjects in this experiment were college students, many of the questions dealt with student problems. The *formal* aspects of the questions, however, are similar to those found in the more usual attitude study.
13. There was one additional question calling for a choice between alternatives. Because it was so different from these 18, however, we have treated it separately. See pp. 64-67 below.
14. The letters here refer to the schedule forms on which this question was asked. These will be explained on

p. 37. The number refers to the question number on the schedule.

15. This is the primary reason why there were no questions dealing with this kind of dilemma. In order to know whether the dilemma really exists one must ascertain, first of all, that the individuals want to achieve the goal toward which the means are directed. Exploration of means dilemmas thus requires two steps; these complications led us to focus our attention on goal dilemmas.
16. These different versions of the 15 questions are reported and discussed in Appendix B.
17. Careful comparison of the three groups obtained in this way reveals no significant differences between them with regard to characteristics which might affect the way in which they answer our questions. We might also indicate at this point that our procedure was somewhat more complicated than we have stated thusfar. Actually six, not three, schedules were used. It will be recalled that this study was carried out with students in the School of General Studies at Columbia and at the University of Washington in Seattle. These two groups of students are so different in many respects that questions applicable to one group would be meaningless to the other. The 18 questions which form the core of our schedule were selected as being meaningful to both groups, with one exception to be noted later. But certain minor questions asked of one group were not asked of the other. Except for these unimportant differences, however, the A form (used at Columbia) and the D form (used in Seattle) are identical. This is true also for the B and E forms, and finally for the C and F forms.
18. This analysis actually was carried out. See pp. 56-59 below.
19. See L.L. Thurstone and E.J. Chave, *The Measurement of Attitudes*. (Chicago, Ill.: University of Chicago Press, 1929.)
20. If similar studies are undertaken in the future, they should undoubtedly make use of more judges in the rating process.
21. It might be well to point out that under certain special conditions this method will not be an appropriate means of judging the relative strength of the alternatives. If, for some reason, one alternative is especially attractive to one-half of the

sample, and only to them, while the second alternative is especially attractive to the other half of the sample, and only to them, then the symmetry of the marginals will *not* indicate equal attractiveness. A situation of this sort might develop if we asked a sample of 50 men and 50 women to choose between two alternatives the desirability of which is somehow determined by sex. Each group would choose the alternative which seemed more attractive to it, but the overall marginal distribution would be one suggesting the equal attractiveness of the alternatives. In concrete cases where one suspects that the symmetry of the marginals represents this situation, rather than equivalence of their attractiveness, further checks must be introduced. The most appropriate one would be an examination of the characteristics of those choosing either alternative. If they are truly equal in attractiveness, the actual choice made at any one time must be dictated almost by chance factors, and the group choosing one must therefore resemble closely the group choosing the other.

22. The value of our scheme should be clear from this analysis. When we know beforehand the relative location of alternatives on one axis, as we did in this case, then the analysis permits us to locate the alternatives on the other axis empirically.
23. The reader should not be deceived by the brevity of this analysis. Each section contains, in summary form, results based on a variety of different questions.
24. This percentage is not average. Rather, it is the proportion of subjects who said in both the first *and* second interviews that they had little difficulty in answering.
25. See Appendix B.
26. Hereafter these patterns will be symbolized by the expression (1, 2, 3; 1, 3, 2) or (1, 2, 3; 2, 1, 3). There is only one way in which there can be complete correspondence; this is represented by the pattern (1, 2, 3; 1, 2, 3). Similarly, there is only one pattern of complete lack of correspondence; this is the pattern (1, 2, 3; 3, 2, 1).
27. This was the total number on which analysis of this kind could be carried out. In three of the 18 choice problems, the corollary question on experienced difficulty was not asked, and three problems were

asked in one form only. This leaves a total of 12 for which there was both more than one set of alternatives and the corollary difficulty question.

28. In line with previous reasoning, the expected values here are 2.5, 5, 5, and 2.5 respectively.

29. This question was originally asked of 179 students, instead of the 128 on whom this analysis is based. However, in studying the reported difficulties, we found that some respondents reported great difficulties on the first interview and little on the second. In order to keep the difficulty groups homogeneous these individuals were eliminated from consideration. "Some or great" difficulty refers to those who reported that this was their experience on *both* interviews; similarly "little" difficulty refers to those respondents who had no trouble on either interview. The index value was separately computed for those who found it more difficult in the second interview than they had in the first to choose between a secure and well-paying job, and for those with exactly the opposite experience. In both cases, the index had a value of .05, indicating an intermediate position.

30. Again we eliminated from consideration those who reported contradictory degrees of difficulty in the two interviews. Our analysis is confined to those who experienced some or great difficulty both times, on the one hand, and those who, on the other hand, experienced little difficulty in either interview.

31. See Patricia L. Kendall and Paul F. Lazarsfeld, *op. cit.*, pp. 148-158, for a discussion of the logic of interpretation.

32. We do not want to intimate that the analysis in terms of predispositions was always revealing. One suggestion made earlier was that we examine decisions between a secure or a well-paying job in the light of varying importance attached to security, on the one hand, and high pay, on the other. The questions which we proposed as a means of locating groups with different predispositions are discussed on p. 40 above. The results of this analysis were so inconsistent that they are difficult to interpret. Our only explanation is that the so-called index questions were not adequate to the task of differentiating varying concerns for either goal.

33. In the following analysis we have combined all three samples of respondents in order to have enough

cases with which to work. This means considering the different versions of the original questions as one. While actually this original form was modified in two ways, the variations in wording were slight and subtle. (See Question 9 in Appendix B.) Analysis of the forms separately shows that we do not distort the results in any obvious or significant way by considering them together.

34. In all three sets, the percentages giving the correct answer increased somewhat from the first to second interview. It may be that some respondents, embarrassed by their lack of information in the first interview, sought out the answer afterwards. If this is true we have evidence of "interview effect;" the experience of being interviewed somehow alters the attitudes or informational level of the respondent.
35. The first set of alternatives provides additional evidence for an interview effect. We notice that the proportion of correct answers increased. Perhaps our subjects were piqued by the hair-splitting distinction, and looked up the correct answer after the first interview.
36. This is a slightly different version of the question asked previously. Originally we asked whether the *same individual* is more unstable in his decision between qualities to which he assigns adjacent rankings than he is in his decision between qualities to which he assigns very different rankings. The question which we have just raised is whether the *same set of alternatives* is answered with less consistency by those who consider the qualities equivalent than it is by those who do not consider them equally important.

CHAPTER 2

1. P.F. Lazarsfeld, "The Change of Opinion During a Political Discussion," *Journal of Applied Psychology* (1939), XXIII, 131-147. This was not a true panel study. Information about pre-stimulus attitudes was obtained through the use of a retrospective question.
2. Some relevant statistical material will be presented in the second part of this chapter.
3. Participating colleges and universities are listed in the Introduction, p. 10.

4. This question was patterned after that used by the Research Branch of the Army in its study of morale during World War II. The exact wording of their question was: "In general, how would you say you feel most of the time, in good spirits, or in low spirits?

   - I am usually in good spirits
   - I am in good spirits some of the time and in low spirits some of the time
   - I am usually in low spirits"
5. The tendency for self ratings to be predominantly positive has been observed in other studies. See, for example, W.A. Bousfield, "The Relationship Between Mood and the Production of Affectively Toned Associates," *Journal of General Psychology* (1950), 42, 67-85. See also H. Cason, "The Learning and Retention of Pleasant and Unpleasant Activities," *Archives of Psychology* (1932) Number 134; and P.T. Young, "Laughing and Weeping, Cheerfulness and Depressions: A Study of Moods Among College Students," *Journal of Social Psychology* (1937) 8, 311-334. This tendency contrasts sharply with that observed in other countries. Following World War II, the *Ladies' Home Journal* asked persons in the United States and Canada and a number of European countries how "happy" they were. In the United States, 46 percent said they were "very happy," 45 percent "fairly happy," and only 8 percent were "unhappy." Very different were the responses obtained from French individuals. Only 9 percent were "very happy," 52 percent were "fairly happy," and a full third - 35 percent - said they were "unhappy." (Quoted in the July 12, 1948 issue of *Life Magazine.)*
6. It is of interest to note that there is less correlation between first and second interview responses to the same mood question than there is between answers to any two mood questions in the same interview.
7. In a later section (see pp. 95-98) we shall find it necessary to adopt a somewhat different, and more detailed, measure of mood change.
8. The details of that analysis will not be reported here. We need only mention that the fit of a latent dichotomy in this instance compares very favorably with that observed in other cases.

9. There were some comments of this sort, however. Consider, for example, "I feel the pressure of too much work; there are only two weeks left;" "There is considerable academic work to be done;" "There are too many assignments to be done and midterms."
10. It might be well to point out that we do not have these expectations with regard to other kinds of attitudes. For example, we know that, in the United States, there is a high correlation between income class and political vote. That is, one's economic status is reflected in party affiliation, just as mood is reflected in certain attitudes. But we do not expect political attitudes to change with every change in income. They are traditional and fixed attitudes, which usually persist throughout the life of the individual. Standing in between political attitudes and those reflecting moods, are, let us say, attitudes toward minority groups. An individual growing up in the South develops a specific set of attitudes toward Negroes; should he move from the South these will persist for some time; but not for as long as do political attitudes under changed conditions. In other words, the time lag between changed conditions and changing attitudes differs according to the traditional character of the attitudes.
11. C.I. Hovland, A.A. Lumsdaine and F.D. Sheffield, *Experiments on Mass Communication*. Studies in Social Psychology in World War II, Volume 3. (Princeton, N.J.: Princeton University Press, 1949) p. 96. Italics added.
12. "Some Social and Psychological Situations Related to Change in Attitude," *Human Relations* (1950) 3, p. 31. See pp. 70-71 for relevant material from the Baltimore Study.
13. Baxter, M.F., Yamada, K. and Washburn, M.F., "Direct Recall of Pleasant and Unpleasant Experiences," *American Journal of Psychology* (1917) 28, 155-157.
14. Laird, D.A., "The Influence of Likes and Dislikes on Memory as Related to Personality," *Journal of Experimental Psychology* (1923) 6, 294-303.
15. W.B. Johnson, "Euphoric and Depressed Moods in Normal Subjects, Parts I and II," *Character and Personality* (1937-38), 6, 79-99 and 188-202.
16. *Op. cit.*
17. *Ibid.*, p. 67.

18. *Workers' Emotions in Shop and Home* (Philadelphia, Pa.: University of Pennsylvania Press, 1932.) There is some evidence that Roethlisberger and Dickson were also aware of the influence of mood in industrial situations. They point out that certain grievances, ostensibly directed toward some person or object, seemed rather to be "expressions of concealed, perhaps unconscious, disturbances in the employee's situation." (*Management and the Worker*, Cambridge, Mass.: Harvard University Press, 1939, p. 266.)
19. *Op. cit.*, Chapter XVI.
20. *Ibid.*, Chapter XIV. This result is very similar to two which we shall present later. See Tables 30 and 31.
21. For the complete list of questions see Appendix C.
22. We can put this somewhat differently; there will be noticeable second order differences within individuals only if there are fairly sizeable first order differences between individuals.
23. This bears on the third assumption discussed on page 90.
24. Table 47 in Appendix C gives the results for the 14 questions individually.
25. We might make one reservation here. For any of a variety of reasons the mood changers may give more favorable responses than the (--) group. We stress therefore that the changers give answers which are similar, but not necessarily exactly the same, as those found in the constant groups.
26. The base figures for these percentages are given in Table 25.
27. See Table 47 in Appendix C.
28. Although it has nothing to do with our main problem, there is one result which is too interesting to be ignored. We tried to keep indefinite the sex of the friend for whom one was waiting. Reactions seemed to differ according to whether the friend was defined as male or female. Thus one student from the New Jersey College for Women said:

    > "I'd wait until I was sure that she (sic) wouldn't show up. Then I'd inquire what had happened."

    Another student from the same college, however, defined the friend as a male, and expressed her indignation at being kept waiting:

28. (continued)

> "I'd wait getting madder and madder. I'd leave after 20 minutes and later inquire what had kept him, letting him know (unless he had a good excuse) that *I didn't appreciate it.*"

A girl who is kept waiting by a boy experiences the situation as more than an annoyance; it is a slight which must not go unnoticed.

29. The wording of the other two is reported in Appendix C.
30. It would have been possible to reword some of these latter questions so that they too placed more emphasis on mood. For example, one question asked "How often do you have the feeling that you would like to 'tell off' the professors with whom you work most closely?" Had we desired to stress mood, we might have worded this in the following way: "At the present moment do you feel that you would like to 'tell off' the professors with whom you work most closely?" This possibility did not occur to us until after the data had been collected, so that we have no questions about college life which parallel those concerning annoying situations.
31. The base figures are found in Table 25.
32. This number is, of course, arbitrary. We could have distinguished a smaller - or a larger - number. For our present purposes, however, this five-step scale of mood change seems most appropriate.
33. Ideally, we should have liked to determine the amount of mood change on all four mood barometers combined. The complications which this involved, however, forced us to consider mood changes on the individual questions only.
34. It might be more precise to say that these questions are *less* likely to depend on one's mood than are items of opinion and attitude. We know that answers to some apparently factual items - education, for example - sometimes seem to reflect the expansiveness of the respondent.

CHAPTER 3

1. Lack of interest could, of course, be defined in a number of other ways. We could say, for example, that someone who has given careful consideration

1. (continued) to a topic and thereafter decided that it was of no special concern should be classified as lacking in interest. The phenomenon of considering a question and then rejecting it is quite different, however, from never having considered it at all. It is only in the latter sense that we shall say that someone is lacking in interest.
2. In one study self-estimates of interest were supplemented by information concerning behavioral manifestations of interest. Elaborate analysis of the data revealed that the self-estimates provided the best single index of interest, and were almost as accurate as an index making use of all of the data.
3. The exact wording of this question was as follows: "Do you think there should eventually be some sort of international control of A-bombs, or should each country remain free to make its own?"
4. The exact wording of the question was: "What do you think are the major issues between the Republicans and Democrats in this year's Presidential election - that is, what things do you think the two parties will be disagreeing about?"
5. This question read: "Do you personally expect that this country will be in another great war within the next ten years or so, or do you think there is a good chance of avoiding it?"
6. We have not controlled education here because it appears to make no difference in this and the following case.
7. This question read: "With which of these four statements do you come closest to agreeing? (1) Labor unions in this country are doing a fine job. (2) While they do make some mistakes, on the whole labor unions are doing more good than harm. (3) Although we need labor unions in this country, they do more harm than good the way they are run now. (4) This country would be better off without any labor unions at all." Respondents selecting either of the first two alternatives were considered to have a pro-union attitude; those selecting either the third or the fourth statement were classified as basically anti-union in perspective.
8. We should perhaps qualify this statement to exclude those cases in which the question is likely to create psychological conflict or ambivalence among those to whom it refers.

9. This question read: "Do you think it would be better to put price controls back on some things, or to let things work out as they are now without price controls?"
10. There are a number of other questions which we might examine. For example, what is the relation between degree of turnover and position of the question on the schedule; what is the relation between degree of turnover and position of an alternative in a checklist; what is the relation between degree of turnover and "open-endedness" of the question? Some of these problems are currently being investigated by Albert Walkley. His data have not yet reached a state of analysis where they can be reported, however.
11. Walkley is making use of a modification of this question in his study. To one group he is presenting an ambiguous statement, "Women should not be allowed to hold high political office." To a second group he is presenting another form which has been made more specific: "Women should not be allowed to become president." The expectation is that those answering the first form will be less stable in their responses.
12. The form in which these questions were finally asked was developed by Mr. Dean Manheimer.
13. See Question #8 in Appendix B. Actually this question was asked in three different forms. Since the same results were observed for each form, however, we have combined them here into a summary table.
14. See Question #29 in Appendix B. Again, this question was asked in three different forms. After establishing that, in each, there was the same relationship between forcing and instability, we combined them into a summary table.
15. We had anticipated that interviewer bias would also bear some relation to the problem being studied. We expected that respondents interviewed by the same interviewer would be subjected to the same biases, and would therefore give more stable responses. These expectations were not borne out by data available in the Cincinnati Study, however.
16. There is no reason to anticipate that these errors of estimation will be biased consistently in any direction; the interviewer will very probably overestimate the income of one respondent and under-

16. (continued) estimate it for another. The random character of these errors thus explains the constancy of the marginals.

APPENDIX A

1. The index was developed by Professor Paul F. Lazarsfeld.
2. $K_1+K_{11}=1$
3. We assume that there is no true change in the opposite direction. This makes sense when we are talking of age changes: it is impossible for anyone really to become younger between two interviews. The same assumption - that true change takes place in one direction only - is not as easily defended when talking about attitudes. Ideally we would have preferred a model permitting us to assume change in both directions. But the model for such latent turnover again has more parameters than can be solved for on the basis of two observations alone.
4. Again we are forced by the limited data to assume that this error is the same in all classes.

APPENDIX B

1. The symmetry is obtained by averaging the responses on the first and second interviews. Thus, the figures 46-54 mean that, on the average, 46 percent of those answering the AD form selected the first alternative; on the average, 20 percent of those answering the BE form did; and, again on the average, 77 percent of those answering the CF form selected the first alternative.
2. These percentages here, and in the examples which follow, refer to the proportions saying, in *both* interviews, that they experienced little difficulty in answering the question.
3. For purposes of studying symmetry and computing the index value, the first two answers were combined as the positive response.
4. Again, the first two answers were combined as the positive response.
5. The last two answers were combined as the positive response.

6. The corollary question on experienced difficulties was not asked in conjunction with these last three questions.

APPENDIX C

1. The one exception to this general statement was Question #23, dealing with the encouragement of classroom discussion. In the second interview, which was generally administered toward the close of the semester, fewer students said that their teachers encouraged this discussion. This finding may reveal an interesting characteristic of teaching methods. It may be that this result reflects the panic experienced by many professors when they realize that they are not going to be able to cover all the material of their course within the available time. They may respond to this panic by discouraging classroom discussion to avoid interruptions of their own presentations.
2. On most questions two or more response categories were combined to give the positive response. Thus in the first question, asking about the student's satisfaction with his school, those answering "very" or "quite" satisfied were grouped together as having favorable attitudes.

APPENDIX D

1. In the Elmira Study, respondents were identified by name so that there was no problem of the kind being considered here.
2. This was not an automatic disqualification of the interview, as some respondents might easily have forgotten the first interview which took place six months earlier.
3. Even though the design of an area sample, such as was used in the Baltimore Study, would be violated by the exclusion of units housing transients, this seems necessary in a panel study, both to cut down mortality and to avoid errors of identification.
4. Indirect evidence for this is that, even among those who were matched on the name of last school attended, there is some turnover on educational levels:

4. (continued)

	Index Value For Turnover in Education
Last school attended same on both ballots	.05
Last school attended different on two ballots	.11

One explanation for this turnover is that some of the cases involving errors in identifaction remain undetected.

5. The two ballots were obtained by different interviewers, which means that there was no consistent bias or falsification on the part of the interviewer.
6. Researchers who have had experience with area sampling techniques report a considerable underenumeration of dwelling units in low-rental areas. See Dean Manheimer and Herbert Hyman, "Interviewer Performance in Area Sampling," *Public Opinion Quarterly*, 13 (1949), 83-92. See esp. Table 2 on p. 86.
7. Even in the Elmira Study, where the panel members were identified by name, there were a handful of cases in which errors in identification occurred.